Making the Most of YOUR MONEY

Making the Most of YOUR MONEY

Louise Botting and Vincent Duggleby

Orbis · London

Acknowledgments
All the cartoons, both inside the book and on the jacket/cover, are © Mel
Calman. They first appeared in volume form in the following books, all
published by Methuen, London: front jacket/cover and pages 22, 35 and 65
How about a little quarrel before bed? (1981); frontispiece and pages 7, 49,
84 and 103 *Help! (1982); and pages 116 and 132 But it's my turn to leave
you . . . (1980).*

First published in Great Britain by Orbis Publishing Limited, London, 1984

Phototypeset by Inforum Ltd, Portsmouth
Printed in Great Britain

ISBN: 0-85613-614-X   hardback
        0-85613-618-2   paperback

Contents

INTRODUCTION

'Money Box', the BBC Radio Four programme, has over a million listeners each week. Some have considerable expertise in personal finance, while others tell us that they love to listen but they understand very little. Most of our audience, however, are people whose knowledge is patchy; they welcome the explanations we give of complex subjects and enjoy the fact that these are highly topical, covering events of the week in a way that they can follow.

They cannot claim familiarity with all aspects of tax, investment, pensions, social security and the many other subjects that we cover week by week yet everyone is going to come up against some, if not all, of these problems at some time during his or her life. It is for them and the thousands of men and women like them that we have written this book. We do not pretend to provide the definitive answer on every subject: this would not be possible in one book nor even in a library of books.

What we have produced is a framework, so that you can begin to think clearly for yourself. A basic understanding of the fundamentals involved will enable you to grasp new financial ideas more quickly, for there will always be new taxes and savings plans, policies and benefits, but you can cope with the variations once you can recognize the theme.

Personal finance is not an easy subject. The problem is that the rules are constantly changing. Sometimes it is simply a new product or a modification of an existing one; sometimes it is an entirely new concept. But as we saw in the 1984 Spring Budget, the first from Mr Nigel Lawson as Chancellor of the Exchequer, there are times when it becomes necessary to go back to fundamentals. As Mr Lawson said when he announced major changes on the taxation of savings and investment: 'The proposals I am about to make will contribute further to the creation of a property-owning and share-owning democracy, in which more decisions are made by individuals rather than by institutions.'

His measures were wide ranging, and included the abolition of life assurance premium relief on new policies, the ending of investment income surcharge, the halving of stamp duty, and the introduction of a new system for taxing bank interest from 1985. 'Taken together', said the Chancellor, 'they will remove biases which have discouraged the individual saver from investing directly in industry. They will reinforce the government's policy of encouraging competition in the financial sector.'

The book looks forward to a new era for savers and investors in the light of Mr Lawson's expressed intention of continuing the process of tax reform over the next few years in the hope, as he put it, 'of making life a little simpler for the taxpayer'. We shall have to wait and see. In the meantime the faint-hearted are best advised to take things slowly if the book seems to get too complicated or sections of it appear irrelevant to your particular circumstances. You can always come back to the subject later, an invitation that we cannot extend to our radio listeners. So do not despair if at first parts of it are rather mysterious; it is not your ignorance that makes it so, but the inordinate complexity of the subject matter.

Although we have tried to keep it all as simple as possible, this is not a book aimed at those who neither know — nor care to find out — what is going on. It is for people who are in search of enough knowledge to do the best they can to protect their families, to save and invest wisely, to pay no more tax than they need, and to understand what is meant by risk. Above all it is for people who are not happy making major decisions without first doing a little homework.

With them in mind, and to the hundreds of people who write to us each week in search of our advice in making the most of their money, we dedicate this book.

I've discovered there's no TAX on lying down and crying...

ABBREVIATIONS APPEARING IN TEXT

APR	annual percentage rate
AVC	additional voluntary contributions
BSA	The Building Societies Association
CGT	capital gains tax
CTT	capital transfer tax
DHSS	Department of Health and Social Security
ERNIE	electronic random number indicator equipment
FIB	family income benefit
GMP	guaranteed minimum pension
IIS	investment income surcharge
INVAC	interest on the investment account
LAPR	life assurance premium relief
MIRAS	mortgage interest relief at source
MWPA	Married Women's Property Act
OTC	over-the-counter market
PAYE	Pay As You Earn
PHI	permanent health insurance
PIAS	Personal Insurance Arbitration Service
RPI	Retail Prices Index
SAYE	Save As You Earn
SEDA	self-employed deferred annuity
USM	unlisted securities market
VAT	value added tax

Chapter 1
MANAGING YOUR MONEY

And give me an estimate for a stamp, please..

There is a common belief that all you need to manage your money is some magic formula; if you are 'in the know' the day-to-day problems simply melt away. Sadly this is not true. Personal finance involves a host of difficult subjects, each requiring some specialist knowledge. Tax planning alone is virtually an industry in Britain, pensions and state benefits remain a mystery to all but the few, while successful investment occupies most of the better minds in the City of London. The problem does not get easier the richer you are. The more money you have, the greater are your options, and you may have to deal with the complex web of capital taxes.

It is often said that a little knowledge is a dangerous thing, especially if it leads to illusions about your own abilities. In personal

9

finance, over-confidence can encourage you to take decisions way beyond your capabilities — and that can lead to disaster. However, acquiring enough knowledge to take an intelligent interest in your financial affairs has excellent results, whether you are dealing with your money personally or using the services of so-called experts and advisers.

A familiarity with the jargon, a basic understanding of our tax law and a general view of the returns available with and without taking risks, enable you to talk the same language as the finance professionals with whom you may have to deal. Once you have a basic working knowledge of the subject, listen carefully; if your adviser cannot properly explain what he is recommending, there must be a suspicion that he does not understand it himself. The use of jargon is a standard trick for concealing ignorance.

Working with the professionals
Britain is not short of financial advisers. Banks, stockbrokers, insurance brokers, accountants, solicitors and a whole collection of other people all involve themselves with varying degrees of skill in managing anything from five thousand to five million pounds. But you must accept that they are rarely impartial, even though they may simply be biased in favour of their own subject. A stockbroker is unlikely to recommend a building society, or an insurance broker favour national savings. On the other hand, the basic motivation of many financial advisers may well be the commission they make from investing your capital in a particular product.

This is not to say that the advice will be bad, but it is worth bearing in mind that the financial world is manned by people of limited expertise who tend to be far more knowledgeable in their own subject than in the general area of financial planning. The only person who will take a continuing long-term interest in your personal finances will be yourself, so the first rule is not to involve yourself in something you cannot understand at the time you set it up, otherwise there will be little hope of being able to disentangle its complexities a few years later, when you will probably have lost touch with your original contact.

Seeking financial advice
There are two approaches to financial advice. One starts from the point of view of the product; the adviser tries to persuade the individual that it is suitable. That is the function of the marketing

department of a bank, building society, or insurance company. It is also the function of the salesman, and in this category you have to include many brokers or 'financial advisers' who are really salesmen in sheep's clothing.

The other approach, though, is to look first at the individual and then shop around for the right policy, plan, investment outlet or benefit to suit that person's requirements. More than half the problem for a good financial adviser is to establish the aims and objectives of the individual; surprisingly, providing the correct advice based on those aims is the easier part of the job. If you can learn enough about how money works yourself, it will be easier for you and your advisers to set down clearly your needs.

The only way you can plan your budget properly is to realize that no single area of your affairs can be taken in a vacuum – they must be taken together, as a whole. In 'Money Box' we receive sometimes hundreds of listeners' letters a week. Often they are cries for help but it is quite extraordinary how often people forget to mention vital information. They ask how to invest £5,000 for maximum income and omit to say that they have a substantial pension. They ask for detailed advice on which the best rate of interest is from a building society, only to add as a postscript that they are non-taxpayers. They ask about life assurance without telling you how old they are, or about tax planning on investments, while forgetting to mention how much capital they have.

Simple money management
Managing your money starts with nothing more complicated than keeping a careful track of what is coming in and going out, matching expenditure to income and hopefully keeping something aside for emergencies. Saving money is merely a matter of putting off spending it until some future date. Saving can be anything from accumulating a few hundred pounds for emergencies to making a long-term commitment to protect yourself against poverty in old age, or even, in its most extreme form, not spending in order to pass money on to your heirs.

Any financial advice, however, must always start by suggesting that you make reasonable allowance for a readily accessible lump sum of cash, probably in the bank or building society. Any adviser who encourages you to put your money into a long-term savings plan before you have made this basic commitment is acting in a most negligent fashion. You will end up having to surrender an endowment policy in order to put a new gear box in your car, or having to cash in some unit trusts because you need to mend the roof on the garden shed after a storm.

Once your emergency fund is sorted out, you can then decide whether to spend or save your income. If you have capital, you must decide how long you want to lock your money up and what your real aim is. Most attitudes are conditioned by two reflexes: convenience and laziness, otherwise why would many people leave hundreds of pounds lying idle in a current account, when they need only £100 or even less to avoid banking charges?

Part of the answer is that they have never got round to thinking about it, but for some people it just does not seem worth the trouble. It may be that in the past they had an overdraft and hated being at the mercy of their bank manager, so now they go to the other extreme by having far too much in the current account. Many people do not even have a bank account at all because they mistrust the system. Others do not bother to look at terms and conditions (admittedly small print usually leaves a great deal to be desired) and then complain because of an unexpected bill for interest or charges. Yet others are suspicious of technology, feeling that outsiders will be able to pry into their affairs or do them down in some way, or that the machines themselves are unreliable. There is another group who place themselves outside the system, still demanding the weekly cash pay-envelope, refusing cheque books, guarantee cards, credit cards, standing orders, direct debits, giro transfers, cash dispensers and a whole lot of new electronic equipment designed to make it easier to handle money. So before we get on to questions of tax planning and investment, the first question to ask is: how much can you save by making full use of these financial services?

There are all sorts of useful schemes, big and little, which can help you. For example, rather than posting bills individually, you can pay them by going to your bank or to the post office and using a single credit transfer through the giro system. This enables you to make a single payment by cheque or in cash which covers all the bills concerned. You could arrange a standing order to put your excess income into a building society account. You could arrange for your bills or rates to be paid regularly by instalments, to avoid the heavy outlay in a particular month which could trigger off bank charges. If you wish to keep several thousands of pounds easily accessible, you could now turn to high-interest bank accounts run by well-known merchant banks and unit trusts, and latterly by building societies and one of the major high street banks. Of course, some people will go to far more trouble than others with this sort of detailed planning. If you decide against it, that is fine; but you must be certain that you are taking a positive decision, rather than just being lazy.

The best way of borrowing
Sensible financial planning also includes establishing a means of borrowing. For many people borrowing simply starts by spending more than they have; for others, any sort of debt is seen as almost immoral although it can represent a very sensible part of an overall financial plan.

For instance, careful use of a credit card, where the borrowing is short term and the account is paid off each month, can be very advantageous since no interest need be incurred. If you need a larger sum for a longer period, you have to compare the interest charged on a bank overdraft, which is usually the cheapest, against a personal loan from the bank or hire purchase. Again, laziness or embarrassment at the point of sale can lead people to take out a hire-purchase agreement, when they could borrow the money much more cheaply direct from their bank. Hire purchase just means filling out a form; bank borrowing might lead to the dreaded interview with the bank manager.

Nowadays, the lender has by law to quote the true rate of interest, known as the *annual percentage rate* (APR), so there is no excuse for making a casual decision to borrow money at 30 per cent when you could have borrowed it at 15 per cent. Remember, too, that whereas you may find yourself being severely penalized when attempting to repay a hire-purchase debt early, paying off a personal loan from the bank early often works to your advantage.

Cleared balances
If you have to write out a large cheque, it is helpful to remember that it takes four or five days for a cheque to go through the system. But you must not let this lead you into a fool's paradise, because it works the other way as well. If you receive a cheque drawn on someone else's account, it may take some time before it actually enters your bank account, even though it may have appeared on your statement. If you are operating anywhere near the point where

bank charges come into operation – usually under £100 in your current account – then it is the *cleared* balance that is critical.

Remember also that computers can make mistakes; computers are only as good as the operators who programme them. If your pay slip looks wrong or your bank statement faulty, there is always a possibility that it is. Check it out and, if in doubt, have the courage of your convictions to query the figure. The Inland Revenue is not yet computerized and openly admit that the number of errors made is legion. Standards are not too bad on PAYE but once you move beyond that – to investment income, capital gains, self-employed earnings or company profits – you really do have to check that everything is right.

Attention to detail is one way you can help yourself; concentrating hard when you make a major decision is another. Getting the big decisions right is critical, such as fixing the right type of mortgage or finding investment outlets or savings plans which suit your tax position and time horizon. But above all else, surround yourself with advisers whom you can both trust and understand.

Thinking about savings and investment

Financial advisers always have to think about the personality of the person they are trying to help. For example, some people will go to endless trouble to increase the return on their money by perhaps a quarter of a percentage point, wriggling through the smallest loopholes to gain what others may see as a marginal advantage, and devoting hours of mental activity where there may be only a matter of pounds at stake. By contrast, others are quite happy to forget both the pence and the pounds, and start to worry only when there are a few noughts on the end.

Before you finalize your own investment plans, you have to decide what sort of person you are. There is no point in wasting time reading newspaper articles and studying tables about what different high street banks charge their customers on current accounts, if you have never even bothered to move your account from the branch of your bank nearest to your first place of work. If you are this type of person you are unlikely to move to the Co-op Bank because they charge less, or from Coutts to Lloyds because they have a lower cleared balance for free banking. Unless your own bank does something outrageously offensive, you will probably assume that competition will ensure that there is little to choose between the major institutions when it comes to the way they treat customers. Equally, if using a strip of expensive postage stamps and a packet of far-from-cheap envelopes just to pay bills makes you angry, you will probably already know that the giro system is one of the most economical ways to handle household bills.

It is just as important not to try satisfying conflicting aims. If you are constantly on the look-out for the best buy in the financial world, do not be tempted to lock up your money for three years by an extra quarter per cent interest, thereby denying yourself the opportunity of taking advantage of a brand new special offer in the coming months. Understand your own foibles. Some people hate paying tax and will go to great lengths to avoid the taxman's clutches. Other people have a fear, irrational or not, that Britain will one day let them down, so feel the need to have funds tucked away in some corner of a foreign land ready for the day they believe will inevitably come when the rich are once again taxed until their pips squeak, and exchange controls are reimposed.

Preparing a financial profile

Financial advice starts by mining for this sort of detail. So why not begin by writing down the answers to the following questions? They should help lead you to the right decisions about your financial plans, and will be invaluable to those who have to deal with your affairs in the event of serious ill health or death.

Personal details   First of all write down your full name and age, and those of your immediate family. Probably the single most important fact in financial planning is the age of the person you are dealing with; equally, a health problem anywhere in the family can materially affect the decisions you take, so make a note of that, if it is relevant.

The home   The next most important thing is your home. Write the correct address down first and then how much the place is worth. What sort of mortgage is outstanding on it, and when was that taken out? Work out what your housing plans are likely to be over the next few years. If you intend to take no action, record that fact. If, of course, no action is possible, be realistic: you may be mortgaged up to the hilt; with a growing family you may need your large and rambling house, despite the fact that you have just fallen in love with the show house in the classy new development round the corner. Are you thinking of moving at any time? Would this mean trading up or trading down, or perhaps moving to a different part of the country where it is not so expensive? Would you have to pay for the move yourself or would your employer help with the costs? Get your time horizon established, even if you will one day change your mind.

For many people moving house involves the greatest financial transaction of their lives. It is the only opportunity that they have of borrowing large amounts of money, and as more and more of the population are now becoming home owners, it is a critical part of what they may have to pass on to their children. Write down an objective description of your home and list what you have done to improve it since you have acquired it.

It does no harm to check around local estate agents to find out what it might be worth. Do not actually ask for a valuation or they might send you a bill, but simply intimate that you might be thinking of selling and would like an outline chat about its market value. Putting a price on a house is anyway more of an art than a science. Once you have it, work out the equity on your house – that is, the value minus the mortgage outstanding.

If you are still living with your parents or in rented property, it will obviously take advance planning to buy your own home. You will need to save, building up a track record for a loan. Facing the problem head-on will serve you better than putting your head in the sand and hoping the problem will go away.

Other assets The next item on the check list is your other assets. It may be that all you need to jot down is a few hundred pounds in a building society, but most people acquire a few things of value over the years and it is very helpful to list exactly what you do have. Old national savings certificates can easily be valued if you get the correct leaflet from the post office; unit trusts, insurance bonds, building society accounts, all throw up a certain amount of documentation. It is worth collecting this together so that you can put down the current value of your various holdings. If this is difficult to calculate, a few letters or phone calls quoting account numbers and policy numbers will fill in any missing details.

For some of you there may be a second home, or valuable furniture or jewellery. Others plough money into a caravan or a boat, and what about your car if it is not provided by the company? Anything that has cost you quite a bit of money becomes an asset, so record the fact. By drawing all this information together, you can develop a sense of perspective. How do your other assets compare with your home – or rather with the equity in your home?

Debts   The mortgage on your house may be only one of your debts. Put down loans against your credit cards, personal loans from the bank, loans against insurance policies or from your employer, hire-purchase or rental agreements, regular outgoings such as gas, electricity, telephone and rates, and any impending debts, not forgetting tax demands, including national insurance – especially if you are self-employed.

Assessing your net income

Now you can begin to prepare a *trial balance*, with assets on the right and liabilities on the left. On the face of it, the difference between the two is your net worth. But your income is part of this calculation too.

Earned income   What do you earn from your job, and what about your husband or wife? Are there any 'perks' on top of your pay that affect your tax position, and save you having to spend your own money? A company car not only cuts down on bills but means you do not have to have several thousand pounds of your own money parked outside your front door. A season-ticket loan enables you to get a bargain. Free private medical cover is much more advantageous than a one-off policy that you have to pay for out of your own pocket.

Unearned income   Earned income and perks come first but what about income from investments, such as building society interest, dividends from stocks and shares or unit trusts, and interest on government securities? Many of these have basic-rate tax deducted at source. Note this fact and remember when doing your tax calculations to add back the tax deducted, so that any liability for higher rates of tax can be calculated.

Calculating your tax position

To help you make investment decisions, you will need to establish your top rate of tax, but before you worry too much about income tax, start with a simple sum, and establish whether or not you are a basic-rate taxpayer.

Basic-rate tax   Put down £2,005 if you are single, and £3,155 if you are married or a single parent. This is the income that you are allowed to have before paying any tax. Add your mortgage interest (but not capital repayments) since this is also tax free. Then add £15,400, which is the current threshold for higher-rate tax. If those three figures added together exceed your income before tax but after pension contributions, then you can relax: higher-rate tax is not your problem. Like most people in this country, you are a basic-rate taxpayer.

Tax for the retired   In Chapter 5 we tell you how to refine this calculation, but for most working couples basic-rate tax is the rule. It is more complicated for the retired. Most people over 65 have extra tax allowances which could mean a tax saving of £145, or £240 for a couple. Remember that the state pension is taxable, and is paid to you before deduction of tax. If that is the only income you have, you may well have no more tax to pay, but these days more and more people have some pension from their job. We will look at how that would be taxed in the light of the state pension later in the book, as well as the particularly nasty tax traps for the elderly that the Inland Revenue will not warn you about in advance (see Chapter 9).

Pensions

If you are not retired, then it is worth allowing a page in this financial profile for the subject of pensions. Very few people understand their potential pension rights and in Chapter 8 we will show you how to extract the relevant information about your pension from your employer. It is only when you have that information you can see the real importance of this part of your financial plan. It may turn out that your pension rights could prove to be worth more than all your assets put together, for a good pension costs thousands and thousands of pounds to provide, which you should relate to savings schemes for your old age which you may be asked to take out, but perhaps can ill afford.

Pensions for the self-employed   The state pension for self-employed people is minimal. To compensate for this, the Inland Revenue has relaxed the rules on how much income can be diverted into future pension rights each year without the payment of tax. The sums are daunting but the principles are clear: if you are not in a pensionable job – even if you do not actually work for yourself – just make a mental note to read Chapter 7 as high priority. Compare your position with someone who has a conventional job. If your skills are in demand, it may be possible to switch from self-employment into a pensionable job in which, with the help of additional voluntary contributions (AVCs), you can solve the problem of income in retirement.

Other benefits   While you are looking at your pension, it also pays to look at what other benefits you are entitled to as a result of your job. For example, what happens if you die before normal retirement date? What protection is there for your family? What if you are off sick for any length of time? Do you benefit under what is known as the Permanent Health Scheme – or, more accurately, the Permanent Disability Scheme?

Insurance

Insurance policies designed to protect your family may be something you have to provide for yourself, but if you are not quite sure it is critically important to establish what you will be worth dead. Remember that all too often these days couples are joint breadwinners yet there is no state pension for widowers. What happens when a wife is disabled or dies may be even more worrying than if the same thing happens to the husband with benefits from his job.

Personal protection   Do not be taken in by the fact that you may be paying out large premiums already on insurance policies. If they are designed for saving, or to pay off the mortgage, they may entail virtually no life cover at all. Pure protection is very cheap for younger people, so write down exactly what you have; if there is the remotest danger that you would leave your family in financial hardship if you died, do more homework on insurance for protection. You will be surprised how little it costs even after the loss of the 15 per cent life assurance premium relief on policies taken out after Budget Day, 13 March 1984.

Property insurance   Remember, too, that the assets you have already listed should also be properly insured. It is foolish to own a beautiful house only to find that if there were a fire, you would be sent right back down one of the snakes of life to start again at the bottom. Building societies only need to protect their loan, not necessarily the full worth of the house, so do not rely on their compulsory insurance requirements; you may be seriously undervalued.

Aims and objectives

By now your personal financial jigsaw should all be falling into place, and you should be able to start writing down your aims and objectives. We are not talking about detailed investment aims at this stage, rather the goals that you have for your life. Are you worried about losing your job? Are you tempted to change career or move house? What are your plans about retirement? What do you feel about your children's education, helping your offspring to set up home, or making a financial contribution towards educating your grandchildren? Do you have tax problems or debts that are pressing? Are you responsible for any elderly relatives, or alternatively are you likely to inherit any money? Many families are now into the second generation of home owners, and whereas once a normal inheritance might be a few hundred pounds and a little bit of jewellery, today we are finding that there may well be a £30,000 family home which is passed on when a widowed mother dies.

These notes you are making are a confidential assessment, so be honest in writing down what your expectations really are. If you have doubts about the contents of your aunt's will, you could try asking. If this would be counter-productive, put a few question marks alongside your answers. Just because you are not certain about every bit of information does not mean you should leave it out. It is much better to put it in and then mark it with an asterisk, if it is only an estimate or an intelligent guess.

Saving for the future   When planning for the future, it may be that you will get a much better return if you average out your savings and make some sort of commitment to a medium-term scheme. But you must be prepared to swim with the tide; a typical plan before the 1984 Budget would have almost certainly included some form of savings plan through life assurance, largely because of the tax benefits. The position now is far less clear cut. For example, a higher-rate taxpayer may still derive some advantage from saving through life assurance on a long-term basis, but for basic-rate taxpayers the Chancellor's underlying message was that you may well do better by standing on your own two feet. Nonetheless be careful never to over-commit yourself or you will quickly live to regret it.

Help and advice
The last page of your financial profile should be devoted to what sort of advisers you have. It really does pay to try and become well connected and well served by both professionals and tradesmen – in every area from doctors to plumbers, decorators to solicitors, car mechanics to insurance brokers. Get into the habit of asking your friends and colleagues if they can recommend people to sort

out your problems, preferably before they become too pressing.

Many people have not got round to making a will because they do not know a solicitor and do not feel like talking to a stranger about their personal matters. Others fail to take out cheap life cover because they do not know who to ask. They are not usually motivated by penny-pinching – saving a few pounds a month at the expense of the family's security; they simply lack the necessary contacts.

Completing your financial profile

Now that the information is all on paper, your next exercise is to stand back for a moment and write an essay on yourself as a financial animal. Try to forget that you are writing about yourself – use the third person. This is the most important part of any financial plan, and is something you can do much better than anyone else. A financial adviser may take between two hours and two days to prepare a similar essay about someone he or she has never met before. Once prepared, however, it ensures that all subsequent decisions fall readily into place.

It is only when your profile is complete that you can start to think sensibly about saving and investment. It should be clear by this stage whether you can afford to save, and, if so, what you should be saving towards. Is it to educate your children or to enable you to buy a better house? Is it simply for next year's holiday or is it because your pension in retirement will be inadequate?

Some people, of course, really do not need to save. Perhaps they have already inherited capital or have a good pension to look forward to. Others may have very considerable financial hurdles to face but few resources to enable them to make sensible provision. However, it is unwise to ignore problems in the hope that they will go away. After all, circumstances do change, jobs do involve promotion, house prices rise and mortgage rates fall, and very often you will find that a problem which a few years back seemed an impossible nightmare, suddenly becomes within your capabilities to solve.

My accountant wants us to stay together..

First considerations

One of the most common mistakes that people make in planning their finances is to choose the wrong outlet for their savings. It is very important to choose a scheme which allows some access in the short term. A classic example is the young couple who commit themselves to a 20-year endowment policy, even though they are thinking of buying a house a couple of years later. Every spare penny they have goes into the policy so that when the time comes to buy the house they have nothing in hand for the deposit, the survey, the legal fees and the removal expenses – never mind carpets and curtains. If they try and surrender the policy they find that virtually all the premiums paid have gone as commission into the pocket of the insurance broker who first sold it to them.

Your age   Another key factor is to find something which is aimed at the right age bracket. Banks and building societies are very keen to make special offers to young savers and, at the other end of the scale, to people approaching retirement, but both groups should make sure they have explored every avenue before committing themselves. Even if you select the right medium, some organizations offer much better value for money than others at different age brackets. Indeed, anything that has to do with life assurance (and that includes most regular saving plans) cannot be judged without reference to age and the critical loss of the 15 per cent premium relief in the March 1984 Budget.

Tax   Then there is your tax position. For basic-rate taxpayers an insurance policy taken out before the 1984 Budget has to run for a minimum of 4 years, otherwise tax relief will be clawed back. But people may now be less inclined to go for early surrender, knowing that any replacement policy will not have tax relief. For high-rate taxpayers there has always been another overriding factor. Their policies have to run for a minimum of 7½ years otherwise there is a liability to higher-rate tax and so in this case timing is still critical for pre- or post-Budget policies. National savings and building society Save As You Earn (SAYE) schemes have been relatively neglected in the last year or so but may come back into fashion, now that the tax attractions of building society linked to life assurance and friendly societies are a thing of the past. The biggest area for tax saving is now without question pension contributions, and self-employed pensions are a must for the higher-paid after a certain age. We devote a whole chapter to pensions but if you are a high-rate taxpayer (or if you are over, say, the age of 50) you should not make any saving commitment without first asking if a pension plan of some sort, or additional voluntary contributions through an existing scheme, would serve your needs better.

Flexibility   Flexibility is, above all, the critical consideration. Fifty years ago the only thing most working people could save for was their burial – the 'penny a week policy' was the earliest regular savings plan. Up to thirty years ago, people saved for the deposit on a house by putting money into a building society; they saved for their old age through an endowment policy. But, with the general increase in living standards, savings schemes have really begun to proliferate. There is now something for every need, every age bracket and every tax bracket; the only problem for you is to choose the right one.

Saving with a building society

One of the great charms of saving with a building society is that it is geared up from the outset to dealing with small savers. Its administration – from the simplicity of the passbook through to the extremely advanced computerization of records – can cope with practically anything. For people who are basic-rate taxpayers and want to establish a convenient way to pay money into their account when they have a bit to spare and draw money out when they need it, there is little to beat a building society. Societies do, however, have special schemes for those who want to make a regular commitment.

Subscription shares   All societies will pay over the odds in interest to people who wish to save regularly out of their pay, and these days that could mean as much as 2½ per cent over the basic building society rate to savers. But be careful; one of the main reasons for saving with a society is to build up a track record for a future mortgage, so do not get tempted into a small society, miles from where you want to live, only to find it is hopelessly unsuitable as a source of mortgage funds when the day comes to buy a house.

Linking with life assurance   The most attractive but least understood of the building society saving schemes used to be the ones which were linked to a life assurance policy. You used to see newspaper advertisements claiming very high returns from building societies – much higher than those available from even the best term shares. Almost invariably these schemes involved linking the building society investment to a life assurance policy and by this means using tax relief on the premiums to boost the ultimate return.

Instead of going into the life assurance company's general investment pool from which bonuses are declared, or being put into units, your money was invested straight back into a special building society account where the interest was rolled up. Most of the big life assurance companies and building societies ran these schemes until they were stopped by the March 1984 Budget. Existing policies, however, still keep the 15 per cent tax relief. Under the old rules the smart thing to do was to surrender them after 4 years and 1 day and take out another one; now people with pre-Budget policies may well find it pays to keep the policy going for the full 10 years.

The schemes were in fact 10-year life policies – and were advertised as such. The return from them depends on the rates of interest paid by the societies over this period, bearing in mind that these are variable and will go up and down in line with interest rates generally. So you might well be asking why the fact that the return was best after 4 years was not made clear. The reason was partly the fear that the Inland Revenue might clamp down on the 15 per cent life assurance premium relief which boosted the return. And this was precisely what happened in the Budget.

Originally it was not possible for elderly people to take out a plan, the highest age limit being around age 65. However, one or two societies did introduce schemes which allowed the elderly to benefit from the building society linked life assurance schemes and at the same time take a regular annual income from them.

Bank savings schemes
Sad to say the banks have lost out hopelessly to the building societies in the last decade in the competition for savings. Various reasons have been advanced – relatively low interest rates, restricted opening hours, unimaginative promotion and a generally stuffy image. There was also the problem of how the interest was taxed and small savers developed a strong preference for the simplicity of a building society account where basic-rate tax was deducted at source.

Ironically the government has now decided, despite strong protest by the banks, to impose tax deduction at source from April 1985. This will be operated in a similar way to building societies, taking a cross-section of savers, making an allowance for those who are non-taxpayers and arriving at what is called a *composite rate*, which will be somewhat below the basic 30 per cent. The problem is that from 1985 non-taxpayers will not be able to reclaim the tax paid and their only option then will be to choose one of the national savings accounts, which have been exempted from the new rules.

Saving for a bank mortgage   Anyone contemplating saving regularly through a bank must have a very specific reason for doing so, and the main reason nowadays is probably the promise of a mortgage. The banks moved into the mortgage market in a big way in 1981–82 and as part of the deal opened up savings accounts which guaranteed mortgages to young couples prepared to save regular monthly sums for a year or two. In addition, when the time came to apply for the mortgage some banks added perks such as reduced survey charges and concessionary terms on hire-purchase loans; and of course these savings schemes could also be registered under the government's Home Loan Scheme, which offers both a grant and a modest interest-free loan top-up during the first 5 years of the mortgage.

It pays to check out bank savings schemes in the light of current market conditions. Most of them cut back their lending sharply in 1983 but increased their allocation for 1984. Even so, total bank lending on mortgages in 1984 is unlikely to exceed £2½–3 billion, compared with the building societies' £22–23 billion.

As well as the banks, one or two building societies also offer guaranteed mortgages linked to savings plans, but the guarantee is only of benefit if there is a mortgage famine when you apply for a loan; otherwise you may find that you can obtain the money cheaper elsewhere. With the building societies now free to go their own ways on interest rates to savers and borrowers, the less you tie yourself up the better.

Any regular savings plan implies a commitment to save for the stated period, and although banks will usually allow small partial withdrawals perhaps once a year the penalty for ceasing payments is usually a much lower rate of interest and a loss of all the 'fringe benefits'.

Children's savings The banks have also made a considerable play for children's savings in the last year or so, offering a wide variety of money boxes, folders, stationery and writing implements as an inducement for eventual teenage loyalty. Most children are not in a position to save regularly – and if they are they may well prefer the National Savings Bank – but there is no harm in checking out the latest incentives dreamed up by the big high street banks, which can on occasions be extremely generous. But it remains to be seen how tax deducted at source affects their thinking on children's accounts.

Friendly societies

One of the fastest-growing savings schemes in the last couple of years was with the friendly societies. The friendly society movement has an honourable history but the type of policy the 'new boys' provided had nothing to do with the Victorian institutions that looked after the welfare of our great-grandparents. The 'new style' friendly societies came into being during the mid-1970s, following changes in the law which enabled them to write tax-free savings policies with modest monthly premiums and a fixed sum assured, which rose to £2,000. That has now been cut back to £750 on policies taken out after the March 1984 Budget.

The advantage of saving in this way was that your money accumulated entirely free of both income tax and capital gains tax, and this was after obtaining life assurance premium relief. The compounding effect of 12 per cent or more a year over the 10-year life of most policies produces a lump sum of between £4,000 and £5,000, which is most unlikely to be matched by any other type of regular savings scheme.

The main drawback was the severe penalties on policies surrendered in the first 10 years, in which case you lose all the interest that has accumulated and are allowed only your premiums back. Once the 10 years' premiums have been paid, you are free to withdraw the lump sum, but in the light of the new £750 limit and the loss of tax relief, many investors may when the time comes prefer to leave their accumulated savings to roll up indefinitely in what will be a unique tax-free fund.

How the friendly societies will develop from now on remains to be seen. The £750 tax exempt policy which can be written by the new style and the traditional friendly societies alike may revert to being no more than a burial policy, but it is possible that by using a combination of joint lives and annuities, they may be able to put together a modest tax-efficient package.

Unit trust savings plans

All unit trust groups offer savings plans; some start as low as £5 a month and offer a means of giving the small investor an exposure to the stock market which would be prohibitively expensive if the individual shares were to be bought in small parcels. It used to be assumed that the only sensible way of saving through unit trusts was via a unit-linked life assurance policy which attracted 15 per cent tax relief on the premiums, and which was used to buy units each month (or year) through a trust. But it was not necessarily the best way of saving if you did not wish to be tied into a long-term plan, and now that life assurance relief has gone and stamp duty has been halved this should give a big boost to direct unit trust savings plans.

'Pound cost averaging'   Timing is the key to investment. The really successful professional will invest far more at the bottom of the market when prices are cheap but rising, whereas the average small investor tends to do the reverse: a run of good news about rising share prices may tempt him or her somewhat belatedly into the market, often very close to the top. With *pound cost averaging* the decision is taken out of your hands. You put in the same amount each month irrespective of unit prices. But you get more units when they are cheap and less when they are expensive.

Tax advantage of unit trusts   As you will see in the next chapter, unit trusts have many advantages for the small investor — one of which is freedom from capital gains tax (CGT) on the activities of the fund; the individual has to realize more than £5,600 of gains in any one year to be liable. A word of caution, though. One snag in dealing with unit trusts through a life policy is that the exemption from CGT which is granted to the individual investor is denied to the insurance company, and when the policy matures unsuspecting investors may well be very upset to see a deduction for CGT from what they thought should have been entirely tax-free returns.

Other considerations   It is probably unwise to choose a highly specialized trust for monthly savings; far better to stick to capital growth or international funds where the managers take responsibility for choosing the right area. Remember, too, that switching from one trust to another can be quite expensive, so make sure when you take on a regular commitment that you will not be indefinitely tied to one particular trust.

The latest idea for getting round the problem of switching costs is to set up what is effectively an *umbrella trust*, sheltering all the different types of fund underneath it. The investor is then able to choose where he wants to be at any given time without incurring capital gains tax or heavy switching costs. As the market for direct investment into unit trusts expands, it is likely this idea will catch on, provided that no objections are raised by the Inland Revenue.

Savings linked to life assurance

The whole question of life assurance used to be intrinsic to regular savings before the Chancellor dropped his bombshell on the industry on 13 March 1984. Before that people in search of protection often found themselves pushed into expensive savings plans by unscrupulous sales people and committed themselves to hundreds of pounds a year where a pound a week would have been quite sufficient to buy protection for a family with young children. From now on protection insurance will stand alone and it may well be that the American maxim will be adopted: 'Take out term and invest the rest.' We deal with protection through term assurance in Chapter 9. Those who did take out policies which combined protection now and investment later through what is known as a *convertible term policy* are in a curious position. The pre-Budget policy continues to attract tax relief, but any increase in the premiums resulting from conversion to endowment or whole life will not get the 15 per cent discount.

Surrendering a policy has always been a bad idea because any profit in the early years tends to be swallowed up by expenses; now the tax relief, once lost, cannot be replaced.

The rules attaching to tax relief on life assurance linked savings were so favourable they prevented far more flexible and equally attractive savings plans coming onto the market. The new era will test the originality and inventiveness of all those involved.

Whole life policies　The longest-term policy on offer is known as a *whole life policy*, because you pay premiums for the whole of your life and the policy only pays up on your death. Before the days of improved widows' benefits and before the move to home ownership and mortgage protection policies, great financial hardship was suffered by widows, who still tend to outlive their husbands by five to ten years. (Even now, there are many elderly widows who have little to live on except means-tested state benefits.) Whole life policies helped many of these widows by guaranteeing them a little extra income for their last years. However, whole life policies are rarely sold nowadays, except for special purposes, such as capital transfer tax planning. In that case they are designed to pay up not when the husband dies but only when his wife follows him to the grave.

Endowment policies　The time horizon on life assurance savings schemes got shorter and shorter; the whole life policy was replaced by the endowment policy designed to mature at a set date in the future. These policies will change in character following the 1984 Budget but they will certainly not disappear. The most vulnerable must be the *non-profit* policy with a guaranteed maturity value. They worked best in a stable world where the insurance company could take a view on interest rates and investment performance for years ahead, but without tax relief the returns are unlikely to be competitive.

It is much more difficult to judge the *with-profits* policy, which is designed to run for as long as 25 years, where investment expertise can prove a critical factor. Certainly the returns have been boosted in the past by tax relief, but the longer the policy runs the less impact this has and high-rate taxpayers in particular will still find them a rewarding outlet.

You take the rough with the smooth, but in recent years these life funds have done very well. The basic guaranteed value of the policy has proved an understatement and year in year out extra bonuses have invariably been attached to with-profits policies, boosting the ultimate value. As a general guideline we can say that a decent with-profits policy will have ensured that your premiums have kept pace with inflation, even through the difficult 1970s.

Unit-linked policies   Some savers preferred something a bit more adventurous than the usual mixture of fixed interest and risk investment; for them the unit-linked policy was invented. For these policies, the premiums are invested in units – be they building society shares, unit trusts, property bonds, or even your own choice of mixed risk investments. The major difference between unit-linked and normal policies is that you get what you buy, the risk is not spread evenly between one policyholder and another.

In fact, unit-linked policies have significantly out-performed the equivalent with-profits policies in recent years. However, it has been an era of rising share prices and there is no guarantee that this will last. And, of course, direct investment through a unit trust has been made significantly more attractive. When you come to surrender a unit-linked policy, you will receive the current value of your units less expenses; if you surrender a with-profits endowment policy, you get what you are given, and that may not be much, if anything, in the early years. The question of early surrender is complicated by the ending of tax relief on life assurance linked savings.

Selling insurance

It is common adage that insurance is sold not bought; whether you deal with a broker or a direct salesman, you must realize that he has a strong financial incentive in the commission he receives to persuade you to spend as much as possible on premiums. His reward comes before yours, and if you change your mind, you will get little in return.

It is a point that is particularly important to remember now there has been a change in the rules on mortgage interest tax relief, which has made endowment policy mortgages relatively attractive compared with the situation before 1983. Endowment policies attached to mortgages tend to be designed for perhaps a 25-year term, yet these days most people move house after not much more than five years. Quite apart from premium relief, you are bound to lose out if you keep surrendering policies every five years, when they have run less than a quarter of their term.

We discuss the choice between repayment mortgages and the endowment type (particularly the low-cost endowment) in Chapter 6. Do not forget, however, that paying out on a relatively large mortgage is effectively a form of saving. You end up with a more valuable house and at retirement you could eventually replace it with a smaller, cheaper home, thus releasing capital for investment.

Saving for school fees

Moving house to an area better served by schools is one way of getting a higher standard of education for your children. It is proving very expensive these days to finance fee-paying education out of income. Endowment policies have often been recommended as a form of saving for schooling but you have to start when the children are very young (between birth and 4 to 5 years) for the scheme to work. By all means look at the sums but remember the basic fact: a good endowment policy simply means your premiums keep pace with inflation, so all you achieve is the spreading of the burden over a greater number of years. You are not being given anything extra, either by the taxman or the insurance company.

Life policies can also be taken out directly for children but tax relief even before the 1984 Budget was not given until they were 12 years old. On top of this, there are legal snags involved in children surrendering policies, except for two companies – Friends Provident and Scottish Equitable – which are allowed by Act of Parliament to insure children's lives (see Chapter 9).

Saving schemes for expatriates

Expatriates never received tax relief, but they may still choose life insurance for saving. The answer for them is to use an 'offshore' insurance company which escapes tax on the fund, unlike home-based companies, which are taxed at 37½ per cent. However, the rules have been tightened up to prevent returning expatriates from converting their savings plans into a lump-sum investment back in Britain while having the benefit of a tax-free fund which remains offshore. In future, they will have to pay basic-rate tax unless the fund bears tax on their behalf.

The new era

It is rare to have such a complete watershed in the savings market as occurred in March 1984, but the Chancellor's commitment was clear that in future he wanted decisions to be made by individuals rather than by institutions and he wanted the merits of the investment to be judged by its performance rather than its ingenuity in tax avoidance. However, until new market forces emerge, we can only focus on those products unchanged by the Budget.

Save As You Earn

Most people associate Save As You Earn with the well-publicized index-linked variety offered through National Savings from 1975 until 31 May 1984. This was, in fact, the third issue of its kind. The original Series 1 contracts were offered between 1969 and 1971, establishing the principle of saving over a fixed number of years and receiving a fixed bonus related to the monthly contributions.

National Savings Yearly Plan   With the fall in inflation people became much less keen on index-linked SAYE. National Savings found themselves paying out £2 for every £1 coming in and so it was decided to withdraw the scheme from the end of May 1984 and replace it with a fixed-interest version called the Yearly Plan. This is still a regular monthly savings plan and it is designed to last for 5 years. The intention is to keep the return broadly in line with other fixed-interest rates; it will be paid free of all tax and need not be declared on tax returns. The maximum monthly saving with the Yearly Plan, which was available from 2 July 1984, is £100 and the minimum is £20. To save on costs of administration National Savings will only accept payment by banker's order. The plan has been designed to give some flexibility and savers can get out after the first year with full interest, but as with national savings certificates the growth is on a rising scale to give holders the incentive to stay in.

Index-linked SAYE Existing holders of third issue SAYE will continue to have their savings linked to the Retail Prices Index, and will be paid back at the end of 5 years. Alternatively there is an option to leave the money invested for a further 2-year term (i.e. to the seventh anniversary) during which no more contributions are made. A bonus of 2 monthly contributions will then be paid, together with full index-linking. There is a further 'extra' in the shape of an annual supplement which was introduced by the government in 1982–83 and continued for 1983–84. It is similar to the supplement on national savings certificates, 2.4 per cent per annum, accruing at 0.2 per cent per month. Breaking a contract still produces a 6 per cent tax-free return (after the 1-year qualifying period) and if inflation continues at a low level this course might be worthwhile.

Building society SAYE Second issue SAYE has nothing to do with national savings; it is offered through building societies, all of whom give precisely the same terms. Anyone over the age of 16 can commit him or herself to put in from £1 to £20 a month over a period of 5 years, making 60 payments in all. The reward is a fixed bonus equivalent to 14 months' payments at the end of 5 years, or by staying in for an extra 2 years (without making any further contributions) a fixed bonus of 28 monthly payments. It is therefore always possible to calculate the return regardless of interest rates (or inflation). Over 5 years you will get 8.3 per cent, over 7 years 8.6 per cent; this return is entirely free of all tax, so to top-rate taxpayers the equivalent would be over 33 per cent. Building society SAYE also offers a useful get-out clause which allows 6 per cent interest on withdrawal between 1 and 5 years, and this is tax free. But it would not be sensible to use it unless rates elsewhere were likely to stay well above 8 per cent. Building society SAYE can also be funded by a lump-sum transfer scheme using an ordinary share account.

Fourth issue SAYE Probably the least-known SAYE contract is the fourth issue, which was introduced in November 1980 to help finance the purchase of shares under employee share option schemes approved by the Inland Revenue. Again the contract has to be for 60 monthly payments over 5 years and this is usually done by deductions from pay.

Contracts taken out before 1 November 1983 qualify for

bonuses equal to 18 monthly payments after 5 years and 36 monthly payments after 7 years, which is rather more generous than the building society SAYE scheme, especially since limits are set higher from £10 to £50 a month, and the fixed return is equivalent to 10.4 per cent and 10.6 per cent respectively.

Contracts taken out after 1 November 1983 qualify for bonuses equal to 14 monthly payments after 5 years and 28 monthly payments after 7 years, so reducing the compound annual returns to 8.3 per cent and 8.62 per cent respectively. Uncompleted contracts which are repaid between year 1 and year 7 qualify for 8 per cent as compared to 6 per cent on building society or index-linked SAYE.

In the 1984 Budget the Chancellor announced an increase in maximum monthly contributions from £50 to £100.

Saving via pension schemes

Few people will regard their pension scheme as an obvious means of regular savings. For a start you have no option but to make the contributions that the employer's scheme dictates, and, secondly, there is no means of getting at the money until you retire. But if you are in pensionable employment, there may be an opportunity to divert your own savings into *additional voluntary contributions* (AVCs) if your employer is prepared to set up a scheme for this purpose. The advantage is that you will get full tax relief on up to 15 per cent of your pay – at higher rates as well as basic – and your money will be invested in a tax-free fund.

The idea is more familiar for the self-employed and those who are not in company schemes. They are allowed to pay 17½ per cent of pay to a personal pension plan. After the age of 50, the proportion allowed with full tax relief rises, to a maximum of 32½ per cent at age 75. Of course, tax has to be paid when the pension is drawn, but that tax may be at a lower rate (particularly for high-rate taxpaying workers), and, more importantly for older people, roughly a quarter of the contributions can be taken as a tax-free lump sum. Effectively, the tax relief is instantaneous.

Saving via pension plans is therefore a strong contender for higher-rate taxpayers, people over the age of 50, and anyone who is worried about income in retirement. It is also an ideal investment for married women, who are allowed the wife's earned income relief against pension bought with their contributions – making a wife's pension tax free up to £38.55 a week.

Chapter 3
NON-RISK LUMP-SUM INVESTMENT

Doctor— I'd like a meaningful relationship with money...

There is no doubt that inflation has been the greatest enemy of investors in the past ten years, and what might be termed non-risk investment is only non-risk in the sense that the capital is returned intact in money terms. What it will buy at the time of return is anybody's guess, as the purchasing power of the interest paid (which may be variable anyway) will diminish over a period of time.

The formula '70 divided by the rate of inflation' tells you how many years it takes for the value of money to halve; so if you assume the rate of inflation is 10 per cent, the value of money halves in 7 years. Alternatively, you can turn the formula round and ask yourself how high the rate of inflation would be if money halved in value every 5 years. The answer is 14 per cent (70 divided by 5). It is also worth noting that the value of money halved between 1972 and 1976, and halved again between 1976 and 1982.

When it comes to safe investment, most people start from what they believe to be a justifiable standpoint. They want security of capital, easy access, proof against inflation and a reasonable income. However, there is no single investment that meets all these criteria without some degree of risk.

Choosing a non-risk plan

The first decision to be made is whether to place the emphasis on income, capital growth or a mixture of the two. Non-risk investment, by definition, tends to favour those who want a regular guaranteed income, and financial institutions are increasingly responding to the demand for income to be paid monthly. A further consideration is the actual worth of the income after tax, and it may well be that drawing off 'income' from growth or from capital gains produces a much higher net return.

When considering the claims of rival products, remember that you will be doing well if you can maintain the 'real' value of your investment and take from it a 'real' return of 2–3 per cent. Do not be misled by salesmen's talk which implies endless growth of 20 per cent or 30 per cent, even if they produce graphs and charts to justify it.

There is often some confusion about 'fixed' income investments as the income may, in fact, be variable, or may vary between different people who invested at different times. Instead it is usual to define an investment in terms of 'fixed interest, variable capital' (such as gilt-edged), 'fixed capital, variable interest' (such as building societies), or 'fixed capital, fixed interest' (as with local authority bonds and certain types of bank deposit). All these fall into the category of non-risk investments – risk investments being usually defined by the variable nature of both capital and income.

Bank deposits

In many respects banks offer the worst of all worlds on any but the shortest timescale, and those with modest amounts of capital (less than £3,000) are usually far better served by national savings or by building societies.

The account most usually quoted as the benchmark is the

deposit account from which money can be withdrawn at 7 days' notice. (It can also be drawn immediately, but with a corresponding loss of interest.) The sole advantage of a bank deposit account over its building society counterpart is about to end. At present the interest is paid gross. From April 1985 tax will be deducted at source. Even now, though, the gross rate of interest is less than the net rate of interest offered by building societies, so it is hard to justify keeping any money on 7-day deposit.

In recognition of this the banks all offer high interest on premium accounts which pay 2 or 3 per cent over the 7-day deposit rate, which itself is fixed by reference to the so-called *base rate* for lending. Originally the only way to obtain these higher interest rates was to use the money markets and for this sums of at least £10,000 were required. The increased competition from the money market funds with minimum deposits as low as £1,000 means the smaller investor can obtain a much better deal.

Types of bank investment account   Banks traditionally offer two types of investment account: one gives a fixed rate of interest provided that you agree to lock your money up for a fixed term; the other will vary the rate of interest according to market conditions and will require a set period of notice, usually between one month and one year. There are some variations on this theme, but your choice depends on your view of interest rates generally. When interest rates are falling, it pays to have a fixed return; if interest rates are rising, the variable rate ensures that the bank does not benefit from your 'cheap' money.

Frequency of interest payments   Apart from the amount you have to invest, the other consideration is the frequency of interest payments. The 7-day notice accounts accrue interest on a half-yearly basis, and unless specified you can assume other accounts will do likewise. A fixed-term deposit, however, will usually have the interest added at the end of the term (if it is less than 6 months) even though you may be allowed to reinvest the money at the same rate of interest. There was a time when the clearing banks enjoyed an advantage over the National Savings Bank in paying interest calculated daily, but from the beginning of 1984 National Savings dropped its old-fashioned monthly calculation to enable withdrawals at any time without loss of interest.

Guarantees against default   Not so long ago, deposits with banks carried no guarantee of protection in the event of default.

This was of little consequence with the major high street names, but the collapse of many of the so-called 'fringe' banks led to a radical reform of the system and the emergence of licensed deposit-takers, subject to Bank of England regulation. The position now is that in the event of default investors are protected to the extent of 75-per cent of a deposit (maximum £10,000). The rules also cover hire purchase finance companies, but not local authorities, or most importantly, offshore banks, which include the Channel Islands and the Isle of Man.

Money funds

The terms *high yield bank account* or *money market account* are often used to describe one of the relatively new developments in the array of financial products. The original money funds were simply a means by which two or three financial institutions could pool smaller sums of money from the public which would not on their own have qualified for wholesale rates of interest. The minimum sums varied from £1,000 to £5,000 and the conditions were broadly similar to ordinary bank 7-day deposit accounts.

The high street banks were slow to respond despite the big disparity in the rates offered, so more money funds were launched by merchant banks, unit trusts and other financial institutions. These started to include such things as cheque books (for minimum withdrawals of £100 or so), standing orders and easy access to investment management via unit trusts and the like. In short they have become a much more useful tool for the relatively affluent to obtain high interest and, when allied to an ordinary bank account, still deal with day-to-day household bills. As a result, early in 1984 the Midland Bank became the first of the big four high street banks to offer a high-interest cheque account paying the equivalent of money market interest on deposits over £2,000, with a minimum cheque of £200.

Building societies

Despite a decade of high inflation, building societies have established themselves as the most popular home for small savers. Their growth has been phenomenal; they had total assets of just under £87 billion at the end of 1983 and it was estimated that 3 out of 5 people in the country had an account of one sort or another.

An illustration of just how badly the banks have lost out to the building societies is shown by the fact that in 1970 building societies held some 35 per cent of savers' money, the banks 44 per cent and national savings 20 per cent; by the end of 1982 the position had swung right round so that the building societies held 48 per cent, the banks had dropped to 37 per cent, and national savings down to 15 per cent.

It is not hard to understand why. The banks had failed miserably to offer competitive interest rates; the building societies stayed open later on weekdays and, more important, were open on Saturday mornings. The huge increase in the number of branches means that you will find at least half a dozen big societies represented on the average high street, and opening an account is simply a matter of walking in, signing a form and depositing your money: modern electronics take care of the rest.

The main criticism of building societies is that they have failed to provide a hedge against inflation. Borrowers have enjoyed windfall gains as property prices roared ahead during the 1970s, while the poor old saver has been left with his capital sadly eroded. Even with interest added back (and not spent) it has been calculated that from 1970–80 the 'real' value of a building society investment was halved by inflation.

As inflation fell from a peak of 25 per cent to around 5 per cent, building societies started to offer not only 'real' returns, but more important 'real' returns after basic-rate tax. Many people are confused by high 'nominal' rates of interest and 'real' returns. The real return is what you get after allowing for inflation, and for well over a hundred years institutions have reckoned that a 'real' rate of 3 per cent was what they should be aiming for. Arguably, if there was no inflation at all, nominal interest rates would be at that level. Bearing in mind this benchmark of 'inflation plus 3 per cent' as a target for pension fund managers and other big financial institutions, by 1983 the societies had started to look extremely good even by comparison with the hitherto untouchable 'granny bonds'.

The other factor which favoured building society investments was the shortage of mortgage money. Over the years there has been a steady rise in the number of savers required to finance each mortgage and the position was further aggravated by the banks deciding to come into the mortgage market in a big way and then suddenly cutting back their commitments. The building societies were left in a dilemma, but, instead of banding together to fight the banks, they ended up fighting among themselves. Rates to savers were ratcheted up, mainly by the second-line societies who saw the opportunity to snatch market share from the big boys, and by the middle of 1983 the so-called 'cartel' (the 34 or so council members of the Building Societies Association) which recommended the basic rate to savers and borrowers was in complete disarray. What emerged was a compromise; the Building Societies Association stayed intact and instead of the 'recommended' rates, we had 'advised' rates.

The result for savers has been to make available a remarkable array of premium share accounts, offering anything up to 2 per cent over the advised share rate and often with very few strings attached. Nonetheless some care is called for in selecting the right account, especially noting any penalties for withdrawal, the frequency of interest rate payments, and whether any differential interest paid over and above the ordinary share rate is guaranteed and, if so, for how long.

Ordinary share accounts   Anyone with a need for quick access will probably use the ordinary share account, in which sums of as little as £1 can be deposited. Big societies all offer the same rate of interest on their ordinary shares, but shopping around the smaller ones should produce at least a half per cent (and sometimes as much as 1 per cent) premium over the advised rate. What the main societies have done is to offer the premium rates either for larger deposits (perhaps a minimum of £500) or to ask for withdrawal notice of 7 days or 1 month. The accounts go by a number of titles, such as 'gold', 'key', 'high interest', 'bonus', 'super', but as long as you are able to hold to the required notice period they offer savers a very competitive deal, especially those with £1,000 or £2,000, who will be able to have their interest paid monthly.

Monthly interest   It is worth pointing out, incidentally, that monthly interest at, say, 8 per cent is equivalent to 8.3 per cent paid once a year. Beware of societies which play this game in reverse and try to kid you into believing that their 'true' rate is really the higher figure; if in doubt remember that building societies usually pay their interest twice yearly. A single payment a year really disguises a slightly lower rate of interest.

Term shares   With that proviso your choice of accounts is really governed by the length of time you are prepared to tie up your money. A few years back, when term shares were being heavily promoted, some investors failed to realize that a 3- or 4-year term meant precisely that; societies were simply not prepared to break the agreement under any circumstances.

Now most societies will allow an early get-out but only with stiff penalties, such as 3 months' loss of interest, which in all probability will leave you little better off than with an ordinary share account, and possibly a lot worse. The advantage of the longer-term shares is that they usually guarantee the differential, whereas short-notice extra-interest accounts rarely do so.

The market now offers accounts ranging from instant withdrawal right up to 5-year terms but it is as well to stress that when a building society talks about 3 months' notice, it means just that, and if you find one that requires both notice and levies a penalty on withdrawals, avoid it and go elsewhere.

Other services   Although the future of building societies as the principal suppliers of housing finance is assured, the trend towards a more competitive range of services is already well established and a new Act of Parliament due in the next couple of years is likely to permit much wider parameters of operation. It is the wish of many of them to provide a one-stop housing service, without the need necessarily to involve other institutions, but whether the societies will be allowed to operate freely in such areas as banking, insurance, hire purchase and estate agency remains to be seen.

Security   A final point on security. In 1982, the Building Societies Association (BSA) established a formal protection scheme which covers up to 90 per cent of an investment in the event of default by societies assenting to it, and 75 per cent for those (including non-BSA members) who have not so far given support. In practice, the big societies have always come to the rescue and have taken over when danger threatened; investors in the New Cross Building Society which was forced to close early in 1984 suffered no losses at all, even though the society did not contribute to the protection scheme.

National Savings

National Savings now offers the widest choice of non-risk investments, ranging from high-yield income bonds to the vastly popular tax-free national savings certificates, with additional access to government securities via their own Stock Register.

The ordinary account   Ironically it is the ordinary account we all grew up with which now looks increasingly uncompetitive. Despite a few fringe benefits which have been tacked on, including standing orders and special arrangements for larger withdrawals, the small saver now gets only 3 per cent interest unless he can manage to keep at least £500 in the account for a full calendar year. Even then the rate is only 6 per cent subject to tax, but with the first £70 of interest tax-free.

A basic-rate taxpayer will do better with a building society ordinary share account; even higher-rate taxpayers will need to do their sums to benefit. The £70 of tax-free interest need not accrue over a full year. Provided the minimum £500 is left in, you could deposit an additional £8,000 for just 1 month – a worthwhile exercise for the top-rate taxpayer.

The investment account   National Savings comes into its own with the investment account, especially since the maddening 'interest on whole months only' rule has given way to daily interest calculations. It is no longer necessary to deposit on the last day of any particular month and withdraw on the first day, though you still have to give a month's notice to get money out.

The investment account is usually the first recommendation for non-taxpayers seeking the best rate of interest and no risk to capital, particularly children (except where the money comes from the parents), and elderly people with only the basic state pension and some of their personal tax allowance to use up. Any amount from £1 to £50,000 may be deposited or withdrawn and the money can be paid in cash at a specified post office or by crossed warrant (the same as a cheque).

Interest on the investment account (or INVAC as it is often termed) is variable and changes are announced by the government from time to time as market conditions dictate. In practice, the account always gives a better return than is available from the high street clearing banks.

National Savings have also bowed to pressure from investors to supply details of interest credited each year without having to return the passbook. This should avoid embarrassment due to interest being omitted from your tax return.

Deposit and income bonds   The investment account, however, does not pay out interest; instead it is credited once a year on 31 December. To get a regular income you need to consider deposit bonds, or better still monthly income bonds. Deposit bonds with half-yearly interest were introduced to compete with building society premium shares, but they lack flexibility and the penalties for withdrawal without 6 months' notice are considerable. Like income bonds, deposit bonds have a 1-year initial term but the minimum deposit is £500, whereas income bonds require a minimum of £2,000; at present the rate of interest is 10 per cent on deposit bonds and income bonds, which is good for non-taxpayers, and they will become almost indispensable when bank interest is taxed at source from April 1985. Basic-rate taxpayers should also consider them as an acceptable alternative to building societies.

Premium bonds   Few people would regard premium bonds as a serious lump-sum investment, but the more you have the greater the chance of winning and the top monthly prize of £250,000 is sufficient excuse for at least £10-worth. Wealthy investors can, in fact, hold up to £10,000 of bonds, but, with odds of 14,000–1 against winning a prize of any sort in the monthly draw, a decent return on the investment is still very much in the lap of ERNIE, the Electronic Random Number Indicator Equipment that churns out the numbers of the lucky recipients.

National savings certificates   By far the most popular of the products offered by National Savings are savings certificates, the main reason being that they are completely free of all tax. This makes them ideal for higher-rate taxpayers, and also for women whose investment income would otherwise be aggregated with that of their husbands and taxed at the latter's highest marginal rate. There is no need for a woman to disclose the fact that she holds certificates and they do not have to be declared on the annual tax return.

The first issue of certificates came out during World War I and we have currently reached the 27th Issue, including the two index-linked varieties, still referred to as 'granny bonds', even though anyone can now hold them. National savings certificates are always restricted to a specified maximum holding expressed as a number of units. In the case of the 27th Issue this is 200 units of £25 each, yielding 7.25 per cent over 5 years. Ordinary national savings certificates carry a fixed and guaranteed yield and, although this is accumulated as growth over the term, there is nothing to stop an investor cashing in a few certificates each year to provide income.

The government decides the yield on the basis of market conditions, and the amount of money it wishes to raise. Accordingly different issues wax and wane in popularity, but you can be sure that if an issue is in really big demand it will soon be withdrawn and replaced by one with a less attractive yield. National savings certificates should not be seen as short-term investments. For a start you need to hold them for at least 1 year to get any return at all (and that includes the index-linked variety); secondly the growth increases year by year so people will not be tempted to cash in early. Once the initial 4- or 5-year term is up, certificates now go over to what are called *common extension terms*, a variable rate of interest, presently 6.84 per cent, still tax-free, which can be compared with other current offers in the market. However, not every certificate has yet moved to common extension terms (and those before the Seventh Issue are not included anyway), so if you have any old certificates check the precise return for the year in question on the tables available from the Post Office.

Index-linked certificates While it is relatively easy to say whether the latest issue of ordinary national savings certificates is or is not a good buy, the same cannot be said of index-linked certificates. This is because you have to guess the rate of inflation a year ahead, and then add in whatever bonus or supplement may be payable (at the present time, this is 2.4 per cent, due in November). The resulting tax-free yield must then be compared with other fixed- and variable-rate investments. The question 'Should I sell my granny bonds?' will always meet with the answer, 'It depends on what you think the rate of inflation will be'; when you bear in mind that the government itself nearly always gets it wrong, you will realize how difficult it is to be precise.

What can be said is that index-linking has served investors extremely well over the years, and those who are not able to follow every twist and turn in the economy may as well relax and stick to their 'granny bonds' in the knowledge that their money is safe and inflation proofed, even if in retrospect they might have achieved a higher return elsewhere. On the other hand, we may be set for a decade of low inflation, when investors can once again look with confidence at orthodox fixed interest or indeed variable interest from building societies to provide a predictable 'real' return.

Government securities

Government securities, or *gilts*, start their life as a means of raising money from the City and the general public for government use. A new issue or *tap stock* is offered at competitive terms, giving a fixed rate of interest, for a fixed period, and a guaranteed promise of capital back at the end. Once the stock is in the hands of the public (or, say, a pension fund or insurance company) it changes its nature. The guarantees from the government of a fixed flow of income and a fixed repayment date can be valued in the light of competing investment outlets – or more novel attempts by the government itself to raise funds.

The risk to capital value   If interest rates rise in general, the flow of income on an older stock will prove less attractive and cannot be sold on for what the original investor paid – whether it is above or below 'par' (usually £100) – so the price falls to the point where the stock yields as much as other new issues. Alternatively, if interest rates fall, the older stock may prove very valuable and be able to command more than par in the market. In general, therefore, falling interest rates lead to rising gilt prices, and vice versa.

Although you get security of income from a government stock, you do not get any security on the capital value of your holding in anything other than a totally stable investment world. The longer your stock has to run before it is guaranteed to be repaid by the government, the greater chance of the price being different from par or the price you paid. You can follow price changes in the *Financial Times* and most other leading national newspapers.

Reducing the risk   To reduce the risk you should go for *short-dated stock*, the issues (many of which are now quite old) which are due to be repaid in under 5 years. *Medium-dated stock* (5–15 years to maturity) can give a higher return but the risk is greater of gilt prices falling on any significant interest rate uplift. The *longs* – over 15 years to maturity – should only be used by those investors who feel confident that other interest rates are on a downward path; private investors can lose out at this end of the gilt market.

Even worse is what is known as the *undated market* – those stocks which the government is under no obligation to repay, such as War Loan and Consols. There are still sad investors who were put into War Loan years ago at 100 and whose holding is now worth a third of what they paid for it in straight money terms, leaving aside inflation.

Index-linked stock   In order to raise money on new stocks, the government always has to offer competitive terms. Interest rates have been so high in the past few years, however, that the government became concerned about the long-term price of borrowing money. While the public may worry about taking on fixed interest securities in times of rising interest rates, the government worry about issuing fixed interest stock when interest rates are falling. It could be paying through the nose for its money (for 20 or 30 years), while investors take handsome capital gains on their stock.

The solution, it seemed, was to issue index-linked stock, where the payment value was not fixed at the outset in money terms but guaranteed to ensure that the capital tied up in the stock over the years maintained its purchasing power. The new-style index-linked stocks simply have a date attached to them when the stock will be repaid at par (100), as increased by inflation. In addition they pay a small return each year and that in itself is indexed.

Since the growth in value in line with inflation is free of all tax, these stocks should have proved the perfect medium for high-rate taxpayers. As yet they are not well understood and have turned out to be less popular than they might have been. They have also been on sale only at a time of falling inflation; it remains to be seen whether demand will pick up if inflation threatens to take us back to double figures.

Local authority bonds

It is not only the government that needs to raise money from the public; local authorities also go regularly into the market.

Town hall bonds   The first are known as town hall bonds; they are often advertised in small boxes in the financial pages of newspapers with relatively attractive rates of interest. This interest is, however, taxable and they are often highly inflexible investments. Where they run for 2, 3 or even 5 years, investors cannot get their capital back except in cases of dire hardship or even, in some cases, death, and what may seem an attractive rate of interest when you take out the bond may prove a considerable disappointment a few years later.

Town hall bonds are fixed-interest versions of the old-style building society term shares. But building societies have abandoned the rigid rules about early surrender and allow investors to opt out, albeit at a penalty. Taxpayers who can take a long view are probably best advised to look to the building societies first, whereas non-taxpayers may be better advised to stick with National Savings.

Yearling bonds For higher-rate taxpayers, though, one of the most flexible investments is a local authority bond known as a yearling. Yearlings raise money on a 1-year view, where interest is paid each 6 months, but the bonds are negotiable, so can be sold through the stock market at any time during the year. The ideal time for high-rate taxpayers is just before the interest is to be paid out, as they can then be sold when the interest is built into the price of the bond, so what would be taxable income is converted into a (hopefully) tax-free gain. In any case, paying capital gains tax at 30 per cent is preferable to a top marginal income tax rate of 60 per cent.

This approach can be used with any gilt-edged security, subject only to fears that the Inland Revenue could question the obvious tax avoidance implications of the action. There was, however, a legal case where the Revenue's powers in this respect were tested, which concluded that if this were done repeatedly the only liability to tax would be according to Section 30 of the 1970 Act, which calls for higher-rate tax, but not basic rate, meaning a maximum of 30 per cent so basic-rate taxpayers can 'bond wash' or 'coupon strip' with impunity.

Just how far investors have developed a taste for this type of tax-free 'income', and to what extent they may switch to yearlings and gilts, is not yet clear, but if Section 30 is abused to any great extent, it will undoubtedly be changed.

Roll-up funds Up to the end of 1983 Channel Island Roll-Up Funds were being used with the permission of the Inland Revenue to convert taxable income into capital gains, to the enormous advantage of high-rate taxpayers. The Revenue became alarmed at the developing market and, from January 1984, closed the loophole, by making the interest taxable.

However, it was not necessary to sell the units and buy them back (known as 'bed and breakfasting') to establish the capital gain; that can be carried forward until the investor finally sells out. From January 1984 interest accrues in a taxable form but that tax is also deferred until a final realization takes place. Thus the roll-up funds may continue to have a use for investors whose tax rate is likely to fall or for those who may be planning to live abroad at some future date.

Annuities

Long-standing tax advantages are also at the heart of another investment – the *annuity*, a low-risk investment of particular value to the elderly. Essentially you hand your money over to an insurance company and it is paid back to you, with interest, for the rest of your life. The taxman, conceding that part of the apparent income is simply a return of capital, allows what is known as the *capital element* to be free of tax. The percentage each year which escapes tax depends on average life expectations.

For a man aged 70, for example, it is just over 9 per cent per annum of capital, on the grounds he should live for about eleven years. Anything over 9 per cent in that example counts as taxable investment income. As the capital element is fixed at the time you take out the annuity, it pays to hold on for as long as possible. The capital element for a man aged 75 is nearly 12 per cent tax-free and at 80 is over 16 per cent.

Annuities are based on fixed-interest returns and can look very good value in time of high interest rates. The annuity dies with you but you can buy a capital-protected annuity to leave something to your family, if you die sooner than expected. You can also ask for a rising income, but essentially what you get depends on prevailing interest rates and the only real winners from an annuity are those who survive beyond the normal expectation of life.

Income bonds   The concept of an annuity has been modified for younger people and turned into what we know as the income bond. Instead of an income for life, the annuity is written as an income for a fixed period. There have been many variations on the income bond theme but do make sure that the person who is selling you one (be it insurance broker or direct salesman) is clever enough to understand them. Be completely honest about your tax position because it can present serious snags. Remember, too, to check just exactly what would happen if you wanted the money out early or if you died.

Many of these income bonds relied on tax relief where part of the annuity was paid into a qualifying life assurance policy to mature after 10 years or be surrendered earlier. Existing bonds, bought before 13 March 1984, will continue to get this tax relief.

Chapter 4
RISK LUMP-SUM INVESTMENT

During the 1970s, people who opted for non-risk lump-sum investment were at the mercy of inflation. Both their capital, and the income they derived from it, were eroded year by year by rising prices. During the last couple of years all that has changed. Savers have been getting real returns – income or growth in excess of inflation, even after basic-rate tax. Ironically, though, as building societies and gilt-edged stock came back into their own, so too did some of the so-called high-risk investments. Stock markets here and around the world boomed and the unit trust industry clocked up record sales.

There were, of course, disappointing areas. Commercial and industrial property suffered badly in the recession; private housing stagnated for a couple of years – values barely keeping pace with inflation in many areas; alternative investment languished. The latter had been the darling of the seventies – where a combination of hobby-style enthusiasm and a certain amount of knowledge could give windfall profits to stamp speculators or busted-bond buffs. The obvious lesson was learnt. If people are not feeling rich enough to buy collectors' items (or they can make money elsewhere, without much expertise), the price simply does not rise.

As the 1980s dawned, it was in the stock market that the real money was to be made. By definition, equity investment means taking risks. When a company raises money it starts with secured borrowing where, if things go wrong, the lender can take back land and buildings. Then there follows a pecking order of security (debentures, unsecured loans, preference shares and so on) but at the end of the line comes the ordinary shareholder, who takes the equity. In bad times the ordinary shareholder may get no dividends at all; if the company goes bust he or she may end up penniless. Conversely, if profits boom, it is the equity investor who scoops the pool.

When company shares are traded on the stock market, investors are not so much interested in what has happened in the past but in what they think will happen next to profits and so to dividends. We often see examples of appalling company news going hand-in-hand with rising share prices, and vice versa. The art of successful investment is therefore not only being able to find out what is going on in industry, the financial world and the economy – but also to get a measure of how other investors view the situation. The question must be asked: how far has the market discounted information? In other words, is the good, or bad, news which is now common knowledge already reflected in the share price by professional investors who have long since made a correct judgement about what was likely to happen?

The unit trust movement

The sheer complexity of investment decisions leads many small investors to enlist the help of professional managers, whose expertise can be bought via unit and investment trusts. The unit trust movement started in the 1930s when investors pooled resources and paid managers to run their investment funds. Each investor had the right to get out at any time and take his proportion of the fund, leaving the manager to sell underlying investments if need be to raise the cash. 1983 saw an unprecedented growth in the unit trust movement; for the first time total assets topped £10 billion, new investment doubled during the year to well over £2 billion and the number of trusts rose inexorably past the six hundred mark.

The very size and complexity of the market, however, brings with it problems for the small investor. Ten years ago it was simply a matter of handing your money over to the chosen fund manager who would then concentrate on income or capital growth, in the main using the British stock market. With exchange controls still firmly in position, demand for overseas investment was relatively limited and what specialization there was had developed in such areas as smaller companies, recovery situations, or commodities.

When exchange controls went out of the window in 1979, it soon became clear that the high-flying unit trusts of the year were likely to be found not among the old-style general funds, but in Australia, Japan or the Far East, in American technology or British gilts; managers realized they could not afford to be unrepresented, if only from a marketing standpoint, in whatever might turn out to be the next boom area. However much they might frown on the monthly performance charts published by the newspapers, having a fund or two in the top twenty did wonders for sales.

At the same time, the emphasis on unit trusts as long-term investment was reduced, and a new breed of intermediaries appeared to advise on a suitable spread of risk among the unit trusts themselves. Only time will tell just how successful some of these services are, and anyone shopping around should satisfy him- or herself beyond all reasonable doubt on the safeguards against fraud and dishonesty, as well as competence and track record. Unit trusts themselves are tightly controlled by legislation in this country, but it is as well to remember that investors in offshore unit trusts do not enjoy anything like the same protection. The best guarantee is usually the name of the organization concerned, especially if it is already operating authorized funds in Britain.

Choosing a trust   Picking the right unit trust is not a matter of sticking a pin in the list of names and hoping for the best. The first and most important thing is for the trust to be operating in the right geographical area. However good the fund manager, he is most unlikely to compensate for a market, or indeed a currency, which is declining. If in doubt, it is best to choose a broadly-based international fund, which gives the managers the opportunity to switch or else stick to British investments.

The second most important decision is to assess the balance between income and capital growth. Most trusts investing overseas — especially in Japan and North America — have minuscule yields (certainly less than 1 per cent) and rely on capital growth for performance. Income funds, which fall into a specialized category, will try to obtain the highest yield consistent with security (but not necessarily growth) of capital. As a group, income funds have not performed particularly well compared with other sectors, but they have to be set against building societies and other fixed-interest investments where there is no capital growth at all.

Once you have made up your mind what your objectives are, it is time to look at the different management groups. It is no coincidence that the same names crop up time after time in the performance tables, and the amount of coverage in the personal finance pages of the national press (as well as various fund management competitions) should leave anyone prepared to do a little homework with a clear idea of the market leaders.

Investment trusts

A different way of enlisting the help of professional management, and spreading risk, is the investment trust. It has a much longer pedigree than the unit trust but there is one fundamental difference. A unit trust, being open-ended, can simply reduce or expand in size to let out, or bring in, investors. On the other hand, an investment trust is a company having a fixed number of shares; if you wish to buy into an investment trust you simply seek out someone who has shares in the trust to sell. The price you pay obviously bears some relation to the value of the underlying asset, but in the final reckoning is dictated by whether there are more buyers or sellers of that particular investment trust's shares on the day you deal.

As a company, an investment trust can borrow at a fixed rate of interest and invest this in the hope that future dividends and capital growth will more than offset the cost of the borrowing. This is called *gearing* (or in the USA, *leverage*). Regardless of how the underlying investments perform, the fixed-interest investors will be looked after first, with the result that ordinary shareholders will do worse in bad times, but when things go well they do better than they would without gearing.

Between World War II and the early 1970s, there was little doubt that shares would (despite their little ups and downs) rise steadily over the years. Investment trusts with gearing became a way of obtaining an even faster long-term rise. In the mid-1970s, however, stock markets round the world suffered a critical shock to the system. Investors realized that gearing increased downside risk as well as upside potential. Investment trusts were suddenly no longer the secure home for widows or orphans but roller-coaster investments best left to the professionals, with the result that more people wanted to sell out than buy in.

The price paid by investors had for years been a little less than the value of the underlying assets but large discounts of up to 30 per cent began to appear, as both private investors and institutions became net sellers. Talk developed of breaking up the old trusts, unitizing them, selling them to pension funds or finding any device that reflected more of the underlying value than simply trading them at a discount in the stock market. The managers, fearful that their role was threatened, decided to fight back, and many followed the unit trust managers' trail.

Helped by the ending of exchange controls and relaxation of capital gains tax rules on internal selling, they began to ditch their traditional portfolios in favour of specialization. The archaic, inappropriate, Victorian-sounding names, once symbols of tradition, were changed to straightforward, informative titles reflecting the modern philosophy. For example, Atlas Electric became TR (Touche Remnant) Technology, and London and Holyrood became Fleming Universal (TR and Fleming being the management groups). Managers also began to convince investors that their expertise should, if not command a premium, at least reduce the discounts on the underlying assets. This reappraisal of their market role coincided with remarkable success in the underlying investments, as stock markets in Britain, America and the Far East reached new peaks. For a time investment trusts did even better in many cases than the equivalent unit trusts.

But which should you choose? Unit trusts will always be easier to buy and sell for an investor who has no ties with a stockbroker. The direct investor will probably use investment trusts as a means of introducing an international flavour to a portfolio, and the very latest trend is to link them to a pension, while the small investor will use unit trusts as an alternative to the building society.

The stock market

Twenty years ago more than half the shares quoted on the London Stock Exchange were owned by individual private investors. As the 1980s got into their stride the figure was down to 28 per cent. This is not to say people did not still have an interest in the market, but it was an indirect interest through pension funds, life assurance and unit trusts. When the Stock Exchange analysed the way share-holdings were distributed in 1983, they found that 26 per cent of the shares were now held by pension funds and 20 per cent by insurance companies, while unit and investment trusts accounted for just over 10 per cent – a total of 57 per cent. In 1975 these institutions held 47 per cent; back in 1963, they held less than 30 per cent. This gives some idea of the increasing power of institutional investment, which was so clearly set out in the voluminous report on the financial institutions of the City by former Labour Prime Minister, Sir Harold (now Lord) Wilson, in the late 1970s.

Soon after, the Office of Fair Trading began a major study to determine whether the Stock Exchange itself amounted to a monopoly, fixing prices to the disadvantage of the investor. In the summer of 1983, the enquiry was halted by the government on the promise by the Stock Exchange to dismantle its rigid commission structure. This is already leading to a substantial reduction in dealing costs for institutional investors, but it remains to be seen whether the small investor will be any better off. In many cases, people who want detailed advice may well have to pay more.

At the same time the Stock Exchange agreed to allow outsiders to take a stake in member firms and almost immediately significant links were forged between banks (both at home and overseas), brokers and jobbers with the aim of providing a global service. The fact that the big investors were doing more of their dealing overseas – especially in the USA – was one of the most compelling arguments put forward to the Chancellor to persuade him to cut the 2 per cent stamp duty to 1 per cent in the Budget.

Direct investment Those with wealth or determination have, of course, been looked after in the City, while the smaller country brokers with less institutional business to rely on have continued to woo those with as little as £5,000 or £10,000 of capital which they can afford to risk in the market. The Stock Exchange itself will always provide a list of brokers prepared to act for small private investors. At the same time, the banks will deal on your behalf (albeit for a fee), provided that you are happy to make most of your own investment decisions. For those with a gambling instinct there is a regular flow of new issues, not least as a result of the government's policy of privatization of such assets as Britoil and Cable and Wireless, with British Telecom and British Airways to come.

Any serious attempt at direct investment, however, will involve a good deal of commitment, not only watching the general trend of the market through the *Financial Times* Ordinary Share Index and other indicators but also the ebb and flow of the various sectors, specific announcements and results from individual companies. There are formulae such as price earnings ratios to be understood, and for those with a technical bent there is a whole school of chart study, where the movement of a share price is plotted to show past reactions, from which future trends can be extrapolated.

How to invest in shares Once you have made up your mind what you want, the actual mechanics of investing are relatively straightforward. Brokers will take instructions over the telephone and these will then be telephoned direct to the floor of the Stock Exchange, where the jobbers (wholesalers, who are allowed to deal only with brokers) will quote the buying and selling price of the shares concerned. Once the broker on the floor has checked the best price available he will strike a bargain with the jobber and from that moment the shares are yours, for better or worse.

The contract note follows a day or two later, indicating the price, the commission that is payable and also the settlement day, which is when you have to pay over the money. The Stock Exchange deals in 2- or 3-week accounts, and settlement is about 10 days after the end of an account. If the share is in a major company, then its progress is easily followed through the City pages of national newspapers, notably the *Financial Times*, whose Ordinary Share Index measures the movements of thirty leading 'blue chip' equities hour by hour.

From the beginning of 1984 investors had the benefit of a new index of one hundred shares which, thanks to the wonders of the electronic age, is continuously updated. The Stock

Exchange '100', as it is called, may well replace the old FT 30 as the main barometer of market trends.

Dividends In the normal course of events dividends will be declared twice a year: an interim and a final. Larger companies may report quarterly figures but these may not be sent direct to shareholders. Whether you bother to attend annual meetings or to send in a proxy vote is entirely up to you, though positive action is required when the company decides to raise fresh money through what is called a rights issue.

Rights issues You may or may not wish to increase your shareholding, but if you do nothing you may find that the value of the rights is lost and your stake in the company diminished. A *scrip* or *bonus issue*, on the other hand, is merely a mechanism for adjusting the value of the shares, usually to make them more marketable. If the price of their shares rises beyond a certain point, some companies believe it is better for more shares to be created and for the price to be correspondingly lowered. It makes no practical difference whether you hold 1,000 shares worth 200p each or 2,000 shares at 100p.

Share 'perks' Some companies quoted on the Stock Exchange offer their shareholders free 'perks', which usually take the form of a discount on the products or services they provide. You may be offered cheap Channel crossings, hotel rooms, dry-cleaning, double-glazing, and a whole range of other things for the few hundred pounds it costs to acquire the minimum qualifying shareholding. While it would make no sense to build an entire portfolio on 'perks', there is certainly no harm in checking what is on offer with your stockbroker (alternatively there is a book published on the subject, see Further Reading in the Appendix). Where the company has good prospects, and you are likely to take advantage of the discount, it could prove a doubly rewarding investment.

Market safeguards Although the Stock Exchange has bowed to parliamentary demands to modify its regulations and allow a greater degree of competition and involvement from outsiders, it has over the years built up an enviable system of self-regulation which governs every aspect of market trading, not least the compensation fund whereby investors are protected against the financial failure of members unable to meet their commitments. The market also requires a great deal of detailed information from the companies which are quoted and there is a special code which governs all takeover bids.

New developments   In recent years the Exchange has had to adjust to new types of business, most notably *traded options* (which give you the right to buy a share at a predetermined price within a specified period of time) and the so-called *unlisted securities market*. The USM is a slight misnomer in that the share prices are listed just like those companies with a full quotation, but the qualifications for entry are less rigorous and fewer shares need to be made available to outside investors.

Financing new ventures   Not every company has to be quoted on the Stock Exchange in order to have its shares bought and sold by the public. In the last few years, there has been another avenue – via the *over-the-counter* market (or OTC) where certain licensed dealers in securities make a 'book' on request. This is often done by newly formed ventures not in a position to meet Stock Exchange regulations, such as making available a minimum percentage of the company's ordinary shares and showing a profits record of at least 5 years, both requirements for a full or USM quotation.

Investment with tax incentives

All this secondary trade in shares does not necessarily divert new money to regenerate industry or help small businesses to expand. In 1981, therefore, the Chancellor of the Exchequer introduced a new concept into taxation.

The Business Start-up Scheme   Anyone wishing to take a modest stake in a brand new venture could get full tax relief against the investment via the Business Start-up Scheme. With maximum tax relief of 75 per cent, the idea was patently open to abuse and it was therefore surrounded with provisos preventing individuals from investing in themselves or their families, and restricting the type of company to one that trades, excluding financial or investment companies. It also required shareholders to stick with the new venture for at least 5 years.

In fact, the restrictions were so numerous and complex that although many high-rate taxpayers found the idea appealing, their accountants warned them off. A year later the Start-up Scheme rules were relaxed a little and the maximum investment was increased. By this time a few funds had also been launched which gave the tax advantages to investors but unitized the holdings to build in a spread of risk, for risk was indeed the name of the game. As any high street bank manager can tell you, new ventures have but a small chance of success, even if they are adequately capitalized from the outset.

The Business Expansion Scheme The Spring Budget of 1983 brought fundamental improvements to the scheme, the two major ones being that each taxpayer could get relief on an investment of up to £40,000 a year, and even more importantly, as long as the shares were newly issued, and the capital went to the company and not to the shareholders, it was irrelevant whether the venture was newly formed or had been around for years. As a result it became known as the Business Expansion Scheme.

Individuals can now buy as much as 30 per cent of the expanded equity and have a seat on the board, as long as they do not receive salaries or directors' fees. If the holding simply maintains its value over the years, the tax relief itself builds in handsome gains, and if the expanded company prospers, it could form a highly tax-efficient investment medium. The risks still deter many investors from taking advantage of this opportunity to develop a direct stake in a company but again business expansion funds have been set up to provide a spread of risk and to give specialist help in the burgeoning venture-capital market. Such funds can however prove expensive to run and you receive tax relief only when the fund invests in the actual company, not when you invest in the fund, so timing can be a problem.

Indeed, no one has any idea yet whether a market will develop adequately to deal in these shares in 5 years' time or so. Minority holdings in private companies are notoriously difficult to value, never mind to sell, and few of these ventures will have developed sufficiently to be ready for the unlisted securities market or even the over-the-counter market. The Business Expansion Scheme entails an act of faith, and so is suitable only for the highest-rate taxpayers, those who really know the venture they are going into and, of course, those who enjoy taking risks with the Inland Revenue's help. From 6 April 1984 the top rate of tax falls to 60 per cent with the scrapping of the 15 per cent investment income surcharge. The Chancellor also saw fit to stop up one loophole in the Business Expansion Scheme which let through investment in farmland.

Forestry Investing in forestry is another form of legal tax avoidance with a much longer history than the Business Expansion Scheme. For many years tax concessions have been permitted to encourage the planting of commercial forestry. You may opt to be taxed under Schedule D, whereby any losses incurred in clearing, planting, maintenance and management can be offset against other taxable income. As the time comes for the trees to be felled, you will be taxed under Schedule B, giving rise only to capital gains tax. You also get *business asset relief*, which by 'roll-over' provisions postpones the payment of CGT by transferring the liability to a new asset of a similar type and, more to the point, halves any liability to capital transfer tax.

Some high-rate taxpayers have invested in industrial buildings and small workshops with considerable tax advantages and yet others use membership of Lloyds. But in all these cases, you need not only a high income but readily available capital which can be tied up for several years. Above all, you must take professional advice, for none of these fields is for the enthusiastic amateur.

Insurance bonds   High-rate taxpayers who seek advice from insurance brokers may also be offered 'single premium' bonds. (Remember that many so-called financial consultants are simply brokers specializing in rich people.) Investment bonds are insurance policies bought with a lump sum rather than a series of regular premiums. The insurance fund can devote all the money to one aspect of investment – equities, cash or deposits, property, agricultural land or overseas investment – or indeed it can offer a mixed spread of investments as a managed fund. These managed funds were very easy to market a few years ago but now have little to offer the general public; today insurance bonds are most often promoted for high-tax avoidance. Investors are given access to several different funds with the right to switch from one to another at little cost and more importantly without technically surrendering their policies. In fact with careful advice, whatever their tax bracket, most investors these days should do better outside the structure of an insurance bond.

Property bonds   One possible exception is the investor who wishes to invest capital in property, when the fund buys the actual property and the investor has a share of the fund. Unit trusts by contrast may not hold a direct stake in property, although this may change if the government accepts the recommendation of Professor Jim Gower in his 1984 report on investor protection.

A property bond not only gives you a spread of risk but enables smaller investors to buy part of something which in the normal way is only dealt in for very large figures. But this fact in itself has led to problems. Imagine two thousand investors each buying a £2,000 bond. This gives the insurance company £4 million to invest, perhaps in a couple of office blocks. It does not quite use up the £4 million, so if some investors want to get out there is a liquid reserve. But if the day comes when quite a few of the investors want their money back (perhaps because they are disappointed in the performance of the fund) the insurance company has no choice but to sell one of their two investments, which can be no easy thing to do in a hurry. Property bond rules therefore permit the insurance company to tell bondholders to wait for up to 6 months.

This clause in the rules has been invoked in the past; it underlines the essential difficulties inherent in any property investment. The difficulties are forgotten when the market is booming, but the recent recession has caused the property market to stagnate in some areas; in some instances investors discovered that photographs of impressive office blocks were far from representative of the investment portfolio. Indeed some bondholders found that their money was tied up in second-grade shops and industrial buildings in geographical areas hard hit by the cutback in the economy.

The end result is that property bonds are less favoured and, since their main claim to fame was that they could match inflation, they may have difficulty in making a come-back. Many investors may feel that an index-linked gilt is an easier road to long-term security.

Tax position Investors in bonds must understand the tax complications. Insurance companies pay the equivalent of basic-rate tax on behalf of their policyholders but exemption from higher-rate tax is only available on what is known as a *qualifying policy*, that is a regular premium policy which runs for 10 years or more. Higher-rate payers are therefore liable to tax above the basic rate, when any other type of policy is surrendered. To tax all the profits as if they arose in the year of surrender might result in an unfair assessment, so the gain is notionally spread over the life of the bond to establish into which tax bracket an average year's gain might take the investor. That rate (minus the basic rate which has already been paid) is then applied to the whole of the gain.

This is called *top slicing*, and by careful income limitation additional tax can be avoided in the year of encashment. Top slicing is not, however, used in determining the 'income limit' for age allowance, which may be lost by those eligible, the over 65s. Partial surrenders (up to 5 per cent of the original value of the holding) are permitted with no tax liability but these rules are misunderstood and it is easy to fall for advertisements and salesmen's jargon which say you can draw off 5 per cent tax free. In fact, the income is tax paid, and be warned also that the higher-rate liability is only deferred and not extinguished.

Commodities

The stock market and property market have attracted more than their fair share of speculators over the years, but nowhere is the speculator in greater evidence than in the commodity markets. Most small investors who wish to have a dabble in commodities should certainly use one of the established British unit trusts which buy and sell shares in commodity trading companies, or possibly an offshore trust which can deal direct in commodities themselves or in commodity futures.

London is only one of the international centres where such metals as gold and silver, copper, lead, tin, zinc, platinum and nickel are traded, along with 'soft' commodities like sugar, cocoa, coffee, rubber, wheat and wool. The underlying idea is to allow producers and consumers to cover their operations, reducing the risk of being caught in a market which is either over-supplied or short of the commodity concerned. In practice, only a fraction of the contracts ever lead to physical delivery and the market is largely dominated by outsiders hoping for a quick 'turn' as prices move up or down.

There have been enormous rises and falls in the value of almost every commodity in the book over the last ten years. Perhaps the most widely followed commodity of all, gold, rose from a mere $40 to well over $800 an ounce. During 1983, cocoa traded between £1,200 and £2,000 and zinc ranged between £420 and £700. It is no exaggeration to say that fortunes can be made and lost overnight in commodities; the commodities market is no place for those without substantial capital and a clear understanding of the very high risk involved. For the inexperienced investor there is also the possibility of falling into the hands of an unscrupulous dealer, for the commodity markets have been slow to recognize the need for a much more rigorous system of investor protection, a point stressed in the Gower Report. It is perhaps worth reiterating the words of a long-time market observer: 'If you feel like investing in commodities, you should go and lie down until the feeling goes away.'

Gold coins and bullion

As far as gold, silver or platinum are concerned, there is always the alternative of buying coins, or indeed bars of metal. The British sovereign and the South African krugerrand are widely held throughout the world, though British investors now suffer the 15 per cent disadvantage of having to pay VAT on a purchase, which cannot then be recovered when selling. The price of gold is fixed twice a day in London and is quoted in US dollars; the coins (rated solely for their bullion value) will carry a small premium on top.

If you are buying and selling in quantity, then you will be able to deal direct with the big bullion houses which make up the London gold market; the minimum limit is usually about £1,000. Alternatively you can use a stockbroker, a bank or your local coin dealer. Commission varies widely, so it is best to get a quote first, and you should also check whether the firm concerned is prepared to buy the coins back.

Apart from VAT, which can be avoided by holding the coins abroad in such tax havens as the Channel Islands, capital gains tax is payable on foreign coins and gold bars (but not sovereigns minted after 1837), although the £5,600 annual exemption limit before realized gains are chargeable should more than take care of this problem. For many people, however, a unit trust investing in gold shares will prove a more rewarding investment, not least because it provides an income and you do not incur charges for storage and insurance.

Alternative investments

Although gold coins are sometimes referred to as an *alternative investment*, more usually it is a term which covers all those items which have attracted the attention of collectors over the years: stamps, other coins, antique china and glass, paintings, furniture and carpets. It is of course possible to make a case for almost anything old to be taken as an investment, but the ultimate test is marketability; hence the main alternatives have been dictated by the activities of auction houses and full-time dealers.

Anyone who sets out to make money from collecting must first acquire a good deal of knowledge. The world is full of gullible buyers and unscrupulous sellers and, as the boom in alternatives collapsed at the end of the 1970s, thousands of people were left with objects whose price bore little or no relationship to their supposed 'value'.

As inflation came down and the stock market went up, money again became available for alternative investment but this time it was based far more on the traditional love of collecting, rather than the hope of a quick profit. Hence the modest recovery in prices of intrinsically rare items has every chance of being sustained.

Overseas investment

After forty years of exchange controls, in 1979 Britain became one of the few countries in the world whose citizens have total freedom to invest wherever they wish. Before then returning expatriates had to close foreign bank accounts and anyone hoping to retire abroad had to claim ill health or accept a modest standard of living as the export of capital was severely restricted. Now the freedom extends to the right to open a bank account anywhere in the world, or indeed to hold foreign currency in a British account. You can invest in a managed currency fund, which is no more than an international deposit account. Or you can buy units in a fund which gives you the right to pick your own currency and switch at will from dollars to Deutschmarks, from yen to Swiss francs.

Buying property abroad   There are now no rules to prevent you buying property abroad, and this has led to a blossoming of the villa trade. But beware. Buying overseas property is a major commitment except for the very rich and in the past many investors have had their fingers burned, often through political problems in the sun spot of their choice – Malta, Cyprus, the Algarve or the Greek islands. There can be local tax and legal snags that also turn such investments into a minefield; not to mention the inherent problems entailed in any property market and the added complication that in such countries as Spain, where the local population favours new houses, the market in secondhand properties has a fundamental weakness that is more reminiscent of the secondhand car market in Britain.

Timesharing   Faced with difficulties in offloading major developments to the hotel trade or private investors, some foreign property speculators have come up with another idea – timesharing. Investors buy a week or two in the villa of their choice, which they use for annual holidays. This brings the price into a range that they can afford and, more to the point, makes the total price of the year more than the speculator could ever have hoped for from one single buyer. Timesharing is still in its early days but many horror stories have already emerged and it is quite clear that the secondary market in partial property holdings will be a nightmare of legal 'small print'. If you have a few thousand pounds to hand, you will almost certainly be better advised to invest the sum safely and use the income to rent for your holidays rather than to commit it to timesharing at this stage in the game, unless you can obtain specialist legal advice.

In general investing overseas compounds the risks and increases the difficulties often out of all recognition. By avoiding British tax you are denying yourself the protection of British law, so tread warily. Even if you are a genuine expatriate, check the true merits of holding offshore units, or using an offshore insurance company. The underlying investment performance is often relatively poor, the choice is limited, and nowadays the tax advantages are restricted to that time when you are actually outside the British tax net.

Taxation serves two distinct purposes in an economy. The first and principal one is to raise money for the government; the second aim is to achieve socially beneficial ends — such as redistributing income from the rich to the poor; persuading people to save for their old age rather than to spend; encouraging them to give up drink or cigarettes, gambling or driving; or to buy their own homes. However, building social engineering into the system often runs in direct opposition to simple revenue-raising. If, for example, the top rates of tax go too high, some people will simply cheat or emigrate. If the duty on a packet of cigarettes is very steep, too many people may give up smoking and thus pay no duty at all. It is the fine balancing of these two

often conflicting aims that has made our tax system so unbe-
lievably complicated.

As the Chancellor, Nigel Lawson, said in his radical, tax-
reforming 1984 Budget: 'I am well aware that the tax reformer's
path is a stony one. Any change in the system is bound at least
in the short term to bring benefits to some and disadvantages
to others. And the disapproval of the latter group tends to be
more audible than the murmurings of satisfaction from the
former, but I do not believe we can afford to opt for the quiet life
and do nothing.'

Our intention here is to explain the basics of the system and
alert you to the point when expert help is needed. An accountant – or 'tax consultant' – is the person to turn to if you have tax
problems; there is no shortage of professionals around with
varying degrees of competence, depending on the complexity
of the problem. There are many definitions of tax, but *personal*
tax should include taxes on income, capital and spending.
What constitutes income tax is a subject for debate because it
depends on whether social security payments should be included. In Britain, our national insurance contributions bite very
hard on the low paid. Combine them with tax, and we appear at
the top of the league table of hardest-hit personal taxpayers in
the West. However, if we leave out national insurance, or look
only at the better-off, we are by no means the highest taxpayers
in Europe, although by any measure we are worse off than our
counterparts in the USA.

National insurance

For those not contracted out of the state scheme, national insurance takes 9 per cent of all income up to £250 a week and nothing
thereafter, so it runs in direct contradiction to the normal progres-
sive income tax system where the rich pay a higher proportion of
their income than the poor. The workings of national insurance
present a very dangerous trap for low-earners, particularly those in
part-time work. You do not pay national insurance if your earnings
are below £34 a week, £4.50 below the level at which a single
person or working wife starts to pay tax.

Income tax, however, only applies to earnings above £38.55 but
national insurance contributions apply to the whole amount. Take a
working wife doing part-time work, earning £40 a week. Her
income tax bill will be a mere 43p a week. But her national

insurance contributions will be £3.60. By earning a mere £1.45 a week over the tax threshold she has to pay over £4 in tax and national insurance. The average working man in this country pays combined tax and national insurance contributions of 39 per cent on extra earnings, whereas a married man earning between £13,000 and £18,555 a year pays only 30 per cent. This is a classic example of the need to raise revenue overriding any socially worthy aims, and it generates a lot of resentment.

Value Added Tax (VAT)

Another tax which leads to a lot of ill-feeling is value added tax. VAT is now our principal tax on spending – although a great deal of revenue also comes from the excise duty on drink and cigarettes, taxes on petrol and the road fund licence for cars.

VAT builds up in stages. At every level of production, manufacture or the provision of services, 15 per cent VAT is applied to the added value before it is sold on to the next link in the chain. By the time it gets to the final consumer, therefore, 15 per cent of the final selling price will have to be added and paid. If the consumer is considered simply to be one of the links in the chain (for example, a company buying raw materials, semi-finished goods or even a typewriter for the office) the VAT can be reclaimed. The only VAT which cannot be reclaimed is that paid by the final consumer – a member of the public.

Zero-rating VAT is simply built into the price of most things we buy and we pay up without question. Some things are exempt, or 'zero-rated', for socially worthy reasons – most food (other than hot take-away food and drink), books, newspapers, children's clothes and so on. Sometimes there are grey areas, most notably in building work.

New building entails no VAT, while repairs and replacements have always been vatable. Between the two lay the massive area of alterations, extensions and home improvements and in the 1984 Budget it was decided to apply VAT to these as well. So whereas such things as double-glazing, central heating, fitted kitchens and bathrooms had been zero-rated, from 1 June 1984 they were brought into the net.

Sometimes a cost-saving can result from a careful choice of firm to take on a particular job. If you hire the services of a large organization to paint your house or mend your car, you will be the last link in the VAT chain and thus have to pay up the full

15 per cent. If, on the other hand, you go to someone who runs a small business, he may not even be liable for VAT. Small organizations – those with a turnover of less than £18,700 a year – are excused VAT simply to save the vast amount of clerical work entailed in bringing everyone into the system, so the small man can quite legally charge less.

It is sensible, therefore, for a customer who is not liable to VAT, and therefore cannot reclaim the VAT he pays, to try and find a supplier who is in the same situation. He will probably be someone whose raw materials form a relatively small part of his price and he would therefore gain little advantage from being in the VAT system. Alternatively, it may be someone who is in the so-called *black economy*, in which case your conscience must be your guide.

The black economy
Because VAT is so very complicated and entails the preparation of quarterly returns (for turnover above £6,200), some self-employed people have chosen not to get involved and simply keep their finances private. They are not happy to have the Excise people (who are not known for their consideration) crawling over their often inadequate books. It may be that quite legally they would be excused VAT because of the small scale of their operations, but ignorance and confusion have reigned amongst small traders, and cheating on VAT has sometimes seemed a simple way of keeping prices down in a highly competitive world.

The snag is, once one tax has been evaded, a trader probably has to evade all the others. Keeping away from the Excise people because of VAT means that small businessmen and 'moonlighters' do not declare their business activities to the Inland Revenue for tax or national insurance contributions. All this has led to a mushrooming of the black economy.

This name derived from the idea that this is work carried out after dark by people (who are in normal employment during the day) 'moonlighting'. There are also people in the black economy whose interest in keeping their activities private derives not so much from avoiding tax as from a desire to protect their right to state benefits such as unemployment benefit and supplementary benefit, which are paid only to those who are not in employment. There have been many estimates of how much the black economy is now costing the country and the current best guess is around £4,000 million a year in lost tax – VAT, income tax and national insurance.

Once you get into the black economy, even in a small way, the nightmares can start. Your business may grow to a level where sooner or later you know you will be caught out, but you dare not own up to the past. The obvious answer is not to hide from the start because in truth the anxiety that is caused by cheating is simply not worth the profits involved. However, if you have been guilty of operating in the black economy, get yourself to an accountant as quickly as possible and put the record straight before everything gets thoroughly out of hand. Most people are surprised to find just how little the price of honesty turns out to be.

Income tax: Pay As You Earn
For the great majority of working people in this country, the payment of tax is automatic and has been since the Pay As You Earn (PAYE) system came into operation in 1944. The PAYE code which you are allocated each year enables your employer to make the necessary deductions from your weekly wage or monthly salary, and it is also the employer's problem to deal with national insurance contributions, which are built into the sets of tax tables.

Assuming that you are employed or in receipt of a pension from your job (90 per cent of those who actually pay tax), then if your code number has been correctly estimated, you will pay the right amount. Under the coding system, your allowances are simply divided into 52 'parcels' (or 12 for monthly-paid employees), and these are set against your pay. The tax tables establish the correct deductions.

How the PAYE code is calculated   Your PAYE code is worked out by adding together all your allowances – specific amounts of income which are set aside from the calculation of your taxable income. For most people these will consist of the personal or age allowance, plus any special allowances for widow's bereavement, dependent relatives, and permissible additions for expenses or loan interest. From this total there may be some deductions for bank interest, but not building society interest (which has basic-rate tax deducted at source), the state pension (which is paid gross) and any adjustment for previous years.

The figure that appears at the bottom of the page represents the amount of tax-free income to which you are entitled, with the final nought knocked off. For example, someone with only the single personal allowance would be coded 200 (that is £2,005 divided by 10 and rounded down). Following the figure will be a letter: L for a single person or wife's earned income allowance; H for a married man; P for the single person's age allowance; V for married age allowance; T for some other type of allowance or when you do not wish your employer to know your precise status, and F if tax is due on your state retirement pension and has to be collected from your other income.

It is the F code which causes the greatest confusion. Pensioners (often single women between the age of 60 and 65 who do not receive the higher age allowance) find out that they are being taxed at the equivalent rate of 34 per cent or 35 per cent on an occupational pension. This is because their allowances are insufficient to cover the other income which they are receiving without deduction of tax. This untaxed income may simply consist of the state pension, but may also include interest on a national savings or bank deposit which the pensioner may have overlooked as part of taxable income.

MIRAS   The major change which took place in the 1983–84 tax year was the introduction of MIRAS (mortgage interest relief at source). Previously the tax relief allowed against mortgage interest was built in through the PAYE system, so those with mortgages had higher code numbers and hence paid less tax on their income. When MIRAS came in, the interest was no longer included in the coding, so people's tax bills went up considerably, while the amount they actually had to pay to the building society went down because the interest was being paid over net of basic-rate tax. In practice, there were various complications, mainly for higher-rate taxpayers entitled to a larger measure of relief than the basic 30 per cent, and at the same time it was decided that anyone with a mortgage over the limit of £25,000 would not be included within MIRAS.

When people came to compare their 'before and after' take-home pay they invariably found a discrepancy. First of all, MIRAS is actually slightly more expensive in the early years than the old 'gross profile' mortgage system; secondly, there was a simultaneous change in personal allowances as a result of the 1983 Budget, and, thirdly, the MIRAS relief limit was raised from £25,000 to £30,000. Although the PAYE system is geared to cope with the usual budget changes to allowances, many people found themselves quite unable to calculate whether they were paying the right amount of tax, and probably will not know until they have completed a tax return for 1984–85.

Adjusting your PAYE code The PAYE system works on the basic assumption that you continue to work in the same job and you continue to qualify for the same allowances. If your circumstances change, then it is your job to tell the Inland Revenue so that your coding can be altered. For example, getting married presents no problem; as soon as the employer is notified of the additional allowance through a notice of coding the tax tables adjust your liability automatically and the rebate will duly appear. When you change your job you receive a P45 form which tells your new employer what your code number is, how much you have earned to date in that year and how much tax you have paid; if you are just starting work then you will be asked to fill in a coding claim form.

The main difficulty arises if you lose your job. Because the allowances are parcelled out by the week or month, when a source of income stops, it is likely that too much tax will have been deducted up to that point. Before unemployment benefit became taxable in 1982, it was simply a matter of notifying the Inland Revenue who repaid the excess tax month by month until you got another job or until the end of the tax year.

Imagine a man had a tax-free allowance of £2,000; he had been earning £8,000 a year, but lost his job after 3 months. His monthly tax deduction would be £150, so he would have paid over £450. But since he had earned only £2,000 gross, if he remained unemployed for the rest of the year, he would have no liability at all, and the Revenue would repay the £450 over the intervening 9 months in equal instalments of £50 a month.

When unemployment benefit came into the tax net, however, the position changed; because the Revenue could no longer be certain just how much tax you might be liable for, rebates within the tax year have been stopped unless, of course, you go back into the PAYE system by getting another job. If you are still unemployed at the end of the tax year (in April), any repayment is worked out and then refunded.

Over the years evidence has shown that, while the PAYE system works effectively enough in practice, there is a 1 in 8 chance of individual taxpayers paying too much or too little tax because of incorrect coding. The message must be: check the code you receive in February or March each year and query any inexplicably sharp change in the tax deducted each month. Budget changes are automatically taken into account by the PAYE system a month or so after they are announced. This usually has the effect of giving a much lower tax bill for the week or month concerned, without any action by the taxpayer being necessary.

Annual tax returns

The other way in which your liability is monitored is through the annual tax return which is sent out every April. In the last few years the Inland Revenue has made an effort to improve the layout of the main types of return form – in particular the new 1984 blue P1 for relatively simple affairs, which won a Plain English award. The brown 11P is for the higher paid or those with income from investments; the self-employed also receive form 11P.

A tax return divides into several sections: some concerned with the income you have received in the past year, some dealing with the allowances and charges which will be used to establish your PAYE coding for the year ahead. Employees are helped by the form P60, which is sent to them by their employers at the end of each tax year and which details earnings, tax, national insurance and contributions to a pension scheme. It does not, however, include details of expenses which may or may not be taxable and unless the employer has a special dispensation, you are obliged to fill in what you have received by way of 'fringe benefits', such as the use of a car, medical insurance, travel and entertainment expenses. The tax treatment of these expenses will vary, depending on whether you fall above or below the £8,500 income level at which you are classified as higher paid.

Not everyone has to fill in a tax return every year. In fact only 1 in 5 of the country's 30 million taxpayers will receive one in 1984. That is not to say that you are being let off the hook. If you believe that you may owe some extra tax – on a part-time job or some untaxed bank interest – then it is your responsibility to notify the Revenue. Not being sent a tax return is no excuse.

Going through the form itself is largely a matter of patience, reading the guidance notes carefully if you are in any doubt as to the information required, keeping proper records of dividends and interest payments, checking what allowances you qualify for; and if your affairs are too complex, handing the whole job over to an accountant. There are many guides to help those prepared to help themselves; the best ones are listed under Further Reading in the Appendix. The Inland Revenue also provides a whole range of free explanatory leaflets.

Bank interest   Probably the commonest pitfall in making a tax return is failing to include bank interest on the assumption that the Revenue will not find out. From April 1985 the banks (apart from National Savings) will have to deduct tax at source, like the building societies. Until that time you should understand the rather complex rules that apply. It is fairly widely known that the banks themselves only make returns if untaxed income exceeds £150 in the year, but they can be required to submit any sum over £15 and periodic spot checks may be carried out. Husbands are, of course, responsible for returning any details of a wife's income, including investments (much to the annoyance of many women); if this is a sensitive issue, the solution for the wife is to keep her savings in national savings certificates which do not have to be disclosed on the tax return.

On the subject of bank interest it is worth explaining briefly the confusing way that tax is assessed on the so-called *preceding year basis*. The Inland Revenue will not know you have opened a bank deposit account until you complete your tax return the following year, so you may well not pay tax until more than 12 months after the event. This tax will be based on the interest you actually receive and the same applies in the second year. From year three, however, the Revenue no longer takes any notice of what interest you actually receive; it looks at what you had in the previous year and uses that figure to decide the tax payable.

In practice the system is not unfair, but many people believe it is because they do not understand it; they also resent the assessment for interest which is sent to them 3 months before the end of the tax year on 1 January, asking for tax on the whole (estimated) amount. To simplify the transition from gross to net payments of bank interest, the Inland Revenue has decided notionally to close and reopen all existing accounts on 5 April 1985.

Taxing a wife's income   Until the early 1970s not only the wife's investment income but also her earned income had to be added to her husband's when making a tax return – with the result that a high-earning couple were so hard hit it even paid to get divorced. Nowadays a couple can elect to be taxed as separate individuals on their earnings. Joint taxation for a working couple provides one married man's allowance, plus one wife's earned income relief, which is equal to the single allowance. If they opt for separate taxation, they each get one single person's allowance apiece. The loss, therefore, with separate taxation is the difference between a married man's allowance on one hand and a single allowance on the other. Currently that difference is £1,150 a year.

It pays to give up £1,150 of allowances when a wife's earnings added to her husband's push the joint income into a higher rate of taxation. By splitting the two incomes, you can save by getting two lots of basic-rate tax entitlement. To find out if it is worth it for you, try both calculations with the help of a simple tax guide or the free leaflet from the Inland Revenue. It does not pay unless in combination you are higher-rate tax-payers; for 1983–84 you needed a combined income of over £22,000 (with wife's earned income of at least £5,680) before it was worth even doing the sums and for 1984–85 £23,800 (with wife's earned income of at least £6,380).

Splitting your income as a couple is known as *separate taxation of wife's earnings*. But in addition there is also what is known as *separate assessment*. This is simply a device to ensure that each partner pays broadly his or her fair share of the combined tax bill, apportioning out the allowances between the couple. If separate taxation is what you are after, remember you have up to 12 months after the end of the tax year to do your sums, so you can apply even after your tax return has gone in. You can also change your mind and revoke an election within the same time limit.

There may be occasions when the wife is the main breadwinner, and she will therefore be entitled to the married woman's allowance plus the married allowance, £2,005 + £3,155. The Inland Revenue, however, may be reluctant to allocate both allowances to the wife to allow her the benefit under the PAYE system unless convinced that her husband really does have no income and no prospect of income. This includes unemployment benefit, which is now taxable. If, in fact, the wife is the breadwinner and the husband stays at home, the family as a whole will pay less tax than vice versa.

74

Returning your form Although there is supposedly a 30-day time limit for sending back your tax return, in practice the Revenue will not bother with reminders for several months. If you allow your affairs to get too far behind, however, interest can be imposed on overdue tax and penalties if there is any suggestion of evasion.

Once your tax liability has been established, you will either receive a rebate, if you have paid too much, or an assessment, if you have paid too little. The latter is most likely if you are liable to higher rates of tax on investment income or to the investment income surcharge, which bites at 15 per cent of investment income over £7,100 for 1983–84. The surcharge is scrapped from 6 April 1984. If the tax due is less than £25, the Revenue may ignore it, and for those in employment or with occupational pensions small amounts of unpaid tax are usually recovered by adjusting the PAYE code.

'Official error' rules Provided that you have supplied all the right information in the first place (and signing the declaration on the front of the tax return binds you to tell the truth), then there is no reason why the Revenue should make any mistakes. On occasions, however, it does happen, and this is where the 'official error' rules may come into play. Since the Inland Revenue can act only on what you declare, you cannot claim official error if you did not do so, which includes not filling in a tax return at all, even if you were not sent one. The Revenue is also given a reasonable amount of time to correct its mistakes, so you cannot complain if you are expected to pay more tax, before the end of the tax year following the one in which the mistake occurred.

After that, however, you will not be liable if your income is below certain limits. At present these limits run from £7,500, under which no tax can be clawed back, on a sliding scale up to £20,500, when you get only 10 per cent remission. For those over 65, or who are getting a state widow's pension, each band is raised by £2,000 (ie £9,500 to £22,500). Inspectors of Taxes also have discretion to give a measure of relief if your gross income marginally exceeds these limits or if you have large or exceptional family responsibilities.

The age allowance It is really important to put the Inland Revenue fully in the picture if you are over 65 and think you might benefit from the age allowance (1984–85: single £2,490, married £3,955). Where either party is over 65 before the end of a tax year, a married couple are entitled to claim the married age allowance in place of normal married allowance, which has the effect of increasing their net income by £240 a year. The age allowance is a concession by the Revenue to all elderly tax-payers except the better-off. If your income is £9,300 or over for 1984–85, you will be back to the ordinary personal tax allowance, the same as a younger couple.

Since it would be unfair to grant the extra £240 benefit in full to those with income under £9,300 but deny it totally to those with over that amount, the Revenue uses a system which is intended to be fair but in fact creates a great deal of confusion. Once income exceeds £8,100, the £240 a year is deducted little by little, by taking off an extra pound for each £5 received. Once a couple's income reaches £9,300, they will have lost all the benefit of age allowance. Looked at from the point of view of the taxpayer, though, 1 pound in 5 means 20 per cent tax, on top of the 30 per cent basic-rate tax that is already payable. Why should a pensioner pay tax of 50 per cent after £8,100 of income – when a younger couple can have well over £28,000 income before getting to a rate of 50 per cent? Sadly those are the rules at the moment.

For single people, the benefit of age allowance is £145, so the run-off begins at £8,100 but, at 1 pound in 5, all the extra has gone by the time income is over £8,828. Single or married, if you are within those brackets, when it comes to investments all you can do is think of yourself as a high-rate taxpayer and act accordingly. The obvious solution might be to place your capital into national savings certificates, where the growth is free of all tax, or to go for low-coupon government securities, designed for capital gains after the first year.

Plan ahead as well, remembering that the state pension (although not taxed at source) has to be added to your other taxable income. Any investment income such as building society interest which is taxed at source and interest on some gilts or dividends will have to be 'grossed-up'. To do this, add back the £30 tax to each £70 you receive, making it £100. You also have to put in the gross value of your occupational pension, not simply the amount you are paid after tax. If it all adds up to around £8,100, then make sure you fully understand the age allowance trap.

Tax and the self-employed

Self-employed people have particular problems over tax because they are not included in the PAYE system. They have to declare their income to the Inland Revenue every year and prepare a list of allowable expenses, which are deducted from gross income. What actually constitutes an 'allowable expense' is for the Revenue to decide. Self-employed people are then taxed on the profits of their trade or profession under what is known as Schedule D. They pay Class 2 and Class 4 national insurance contributions, instead of the Class 1 applicable to the employed.

Since the self-employed are allowed to pay their tax in arrears (often more than a year after the money has been earned), they have undoubted cash flow advantages over their conventionally employed colleagues. On the other hand, tax bills always seem to come as a nasty shock to those on Schedule D — it is rare to meet someone who makes careful provision for the inevitable bill. Most self-employed people use the services of a professional accountant (whose fees are usually an allowable expense in themselves), so the simplest safeguard against unexpected tax bills is to ask your accountant to do a back-of-the-envelope estimate for your current tax; it may be unrealistic to imagine that you will save the correct amount month by month but at least you will have an idea of whether or not you can afford a holiday.

Using an accountant   A good accountant will also explain what spending is tax-efficient — travel, motoring, equipment, postage and so on — and what is coming out of your after-tax income, such as entertainment. He will also indicate to you what scope there is for such things as self-employed pension contributions, which we describe in Chapter 7. Most of all he will be able to prepare a set of accounts for the Inland Revenue which will encourage the impression that you have the running of your business in some sort of order. Most accountants are more familiar with the affairs of the self-employed than those in conventional employment, whose tax is dealt with through the PAYE system and who often have no need of professional help.

Maximizing your overall tax position

Whether you have an accountant or not, some overall look at the tax you are paying each year never comes amiss. As far as earnings are concerned, there is not much room for manoeuvre.

Pension schemes   For the self-employed and those not in rigid pension schemes, it may be possible to offset additional pension contributions against earned income; for directors of small companies, the purchase of extra pension rights may be a sensible alternative to a bonus; the self-employed can offset these for 6 years.

The company car   For those with a company motor car, remember that mileage may affect the tax assessment. With business mileage of 2,500 miles or less you will pay 50 per cent more than the scale rate, whereas if you drive 18,000 miles or more your tax liability will be halved (see the Tables in the Appendix). It could pay to drive your car to the next few meetings rather than take a train.

Foreign travel   For those who go further afield, foreign travel allowance used to save tax on 25 per cent of your earnings attributable to the work you do overseas, but only if you were abroad for more than 30 days. That concession has been reduced to 12½ per cent for 1984–85 and scrapped thereafter. An overseas trip organized for this tax year rather than next could just pay on tax saving.

Student covenants   Parents with student sons or daughters over the age of 18 could organize a covenant. A *deed of covenant* is a legal agreement under which one person promises to make a regular series of payments to someone else. The necessary forms can be prepared by a solicitor, or you can do it yourself with the help of a pre-printed form such as that produced for students by the Inland Revenue (form IR47). For tax purposes, the parents deduct basic-rate tax which the students can then reclaim, as long as the gross covenant is below their personal tax allowance. Anyone other than a parent can do the same for younger children, but it must be capable of lasting 7 years. Although the covenant will obviously be cancelled once the recipient has a high enough income to be a taxpayer in his or her own right, the Revenue does not seek to get the tax back.

Charity covenants   You can get higher-rate tax relief on a covenant up to £5,000 a year, if the gift is for charity. Covenants to charities have to last for 4 years, but a simple advance payment on a 4-year covenant can enable the charity to receive all the gift at once, although the taxpayer gets the relief year by year for the next 4 years.

Life assurance and mortgage interest   Until quite recently tax relief on life assurance and mortgage interest were ways of cutting down your tax bill. Oddly enough, nowadays you do not need to be a taxpayer to get mortgage interest relief since it is given automatically at source; so is life assurance premium relief for United Kingdom pre-Budget policies. At the end of the book we give you a list of Further Reading, and if you feel you are paying too much tax on your earnings it could be worth doing more homework or going to an accountant for advice, even if you are within the PAYE scheme. However, the real scope for tax avoidance comes not so much with earnings as with capital.

Investment income surcharge   Under the old tax rules, interest and dividends were taxed at the same rate as earned income, unless they exceeded £7,100 after deducting mortgage interest payments. At this point the investment income surcharge began to bite, increasing the marginal tax rate by 15 per cent. Thus, while the top rate of tax on earned income was 60 per cent, the top rate on unearned income was 75 per cent. So the incentive to convert income of this type into capital gains, where the rate is only 30 per cent, was considerable. The fact that the investment income surcharge was avoidable was one reason the Chancellor scrapped it from April 1984.

Taxes on capital

For most people, taxes on capital mean *capital gains tax*, (CGT) which is charged on the growth in the value of certain realized assets and *capital transfer tax* (CTT), which is tax covering lifetime gifts and bequests on death, except those between husband and wife, but subject to certain exemptions. We are not concerned here with development land tax, which requires specialist advice and starts at £75,000.

Capital gains tax   CGT has aroused considerable resentment since it was first introduced in 1965. The main reason is that it has proved to be a tax on inflation and thus effectively a wealth tax. For example, if you hold an asset which doubles in value over a period when the value of money has halved, you make no real gain when you sell; yet until recently, you could have been charged 30 per cent CGT on the monetary gain, meaning that you could end up losing one sixth of the real value of an asset which has merely kept pace with inflation.

The severity of this backdoor wealth tax became increasingly apparent in the era of very high inflation in the 1970s and various devices were brought in to overcome it. First, year by year the level at which capital gains tax applied has been lifted, and CGT now only applies on realized chargeable gains of over £5,600 a year. Such things as unit and investment trusts no longer suffer CGT internally on their funds.

But most important was the reform brought in from April 1982 which allowed gains after the first year to be liable to CGT only in so far as they exceed the rate of inflation. On newly bought assets, such as shares or a second home, this could prove a great saving. Sadly, though, the indexation applies to the original purchase price rather than the 1982 value, so assets bought years ago still suffer. Nevertheless it has possibilities. For example, you can give your second home to your son or daughter, with a large contingent liability to CGT, but the tax liability can be passed on, so that the recipient assumes a liability for the gain that has built up. Although it will have been acquired at its original value, if the person then occupies the property as his or her principal private residence, there will be no CGT to pay because any profit on a main residence is exempt from tax.

CGT exemptions   The *principal private residence exemption* has been there from the outset. It applies to your home and, if you own two or more properties, you are allowed to elect which is your principal residence. You are also allowed to leave it empty or let it to tenants if you go abroad to work for any length of time, or for up to 4 years if your job takes you elsewhere in Britain, without losing the exemption. You are anyway allowed periods of absence totalling 3 years for whatever reason and you are now allowed a couple of years at the end when you are moving house, before the old home becomes liable to CGT.

The self-employed should watch out here if they work from home. Capital gains tax can apply to any part of the house which is specifically set aside for work – an office, a surgery, a garage or whatever. If, however, you work at the kitchen table, entertain business contacts in your sitting room and use a bedroom occasionally as a study, you should have no problem.

There are other gains which are exempt from CGT altogether, most notable being the increase in value in government securities, and certain newly-issued corporate bonds, held for more than 12 months and gains on chattels (anything from motor cars not used for business, to furniture, pictures, jewellery or even domestic animals) sold for £3,000 or less. Growth in insurance policies is normally exempt, except with some unit-linked policies where the life fund does not pay the CGT but leaves the policyholder to pay on maturity. Anyone spending a full tax year or longer overseas should take expert advice if he or she holds assets with a contingent liability to CGT on them, since realizations may escape CGT totally if sold at the correct time.

CGT on sales of assets   CGT may be payable on sales of assets used in a business, unless you spend the proceeds replacing them with further assets for the business, when the tax liability can be rolled over (passed on). If you are over 65 and you sell (or give away) a business you have owned for more than 10 years, you may be allowed to ignore the first £100,000 of gain. This *business retirement relief* also applies to shares in a family company where you have at least 25 per cent of the voting rights, or your family has at least 51 per cent including 5 per cent or more for you. Over the age of 60, scaled-down business retirement relief may be available, and the whole question of this relief is under review and may be improved.

Capital transfer tax   For most people capital transfer tax is more of a threat than a reality. When it replaced the old estate duty from March 1975, the aim was to scrap what had been an avoidable tax, in that you could give away as much as you liked and pay nothing if you survived 7 years, and substitute something which depended not on timing but on the cumulative amount given away. The actual transfer triggered the tax, *inter vivos* (between living persons) or on death. It was therefore somewhat ironic that a subsequent modification of CTT reintroduced the time concept, so that gifts made more than 10 years previously now drop out of the cumulative reckoning.

CTT exemptions   There are tax-free exemptions to CTT: just one of the various ways by which the government allows people to mitigate the effect of the tax. Most notable is the freedom to pass assets between husband and wife without any liability. Married couples apart, the exemptions enable anyone to pass on up to £64,000 of his or her wealth tax-free – an exercise that can be repeated every 10 years if required. Apart from that £3,000 can be passed on every year (an exemption which can be carried forward one year only), plus £250 a year to as many individuals as you wish; in addition any further amount that can be given away out of income without affecting your usual lifestyle is exempt, plus various one-off gifts on marriage, depending on your relationship to the person involved.

In practice it will be seen that those of modest means (even if that includes a house) have nothing to worry about. If none of the £64,000 exemption has been used in your lifetime, then it is available on your death, though it should be made clear that if you do give away assets above this level then the lifetime rate of tax starts at only 15 per cent, compared with 30 per cent on death (or gifts within three years of death).

The 1984 Budget contained a major revision of the rates, because in the Chancellor's view our highest rates of capital transfer tax were far too high and badly out of line with comparable rates abroad. As a result he reduced the top rate of tax to 60 per cent, payable only on estates over £285,000. He also simplified the scale for lifetime gifts so that it is now always half that on death. The combined effect of these two measures produces a top rate of 30 per cent on lifetime gifts. (See Appendix for tables.)

These bands are reviewed every year in the Budget and the thresholds are automatically increased by the rate of inflation, unless the Chancellor of the Exchequer decides otherwise.

Insurance exemptions Insurance has always played a big part in estate planning. Prior to 1975, policies written under the Married Women's Property Act (MWPA) were widely used to avoid duty on the first death, but the advent of capital transfer tax made the MWPA largely irrelevant because a husband could transfer as much property as he wished to his wife, or vice versa, without paying CTT. (Previously, wives had to pay estate duty on the value of property left to them by their husbands. Since this often included the marital home, it was a thoroughly unjust levy, which meant women were often left with little or no means of providing an income for themselves.) However, it may still be worth writing a life policy on trust for the children, bearing in mind that the expenditure usually comes out of income, and over a period of 20 years or so a substantial sum will have built up.

In the past few years, however, insurance companies have set up a variety of more sophisticated CTT avoidance schemes, under the collective title of *inheritance trusts*. Opinion is divided on their merits and they are certainly not cheap since they are mostly based on insurance bonds and therefore attract a hefty chunk of commission.

Inheritance trusts rely heavily on the 10-yearly exemption of £64,000 and the annual exemption of £3,000. Some combine these with an interest-free loan either to or from the donor, but the end result is to have the money 'rolled up' in an investment bond administered by the insurance company, so that all the subsequent growth accrues to the beneficiaries. The trusts can be constructed with a variety of options so that donors can allow for changing circumstances – premature death, or even divorce, as well as keeping a regular income for themselves. This is *not* an area in which to get involved without independent professional advice as some schemes take several years to become fully effective and are always vulnerable to sudden changes in tax law.

The best form of CTT planning for husbands and wives at any stage of their lives is to equalize their assets, maximizing the tax-free concessions available to both partners. This includes an owner-occupied house, but here it could pay to go not for a joint tenancy, where on death the whole property passes to the surviving spouse, but for a tenancy in common, which enables half the house to be transferred to the next generation when one partner dies. However, the idea of transferring property bit by bit to your heirs (sometimes called a *salami scheme*) can lead to unforeseen problems over stamp duty and capital gains tax and once again should only be contemplated with professional help.

There are other means of reducing the ultimate CTT bill for the wealthy, such as investing in farmland or woodland, which can sometimes qualify for a 50 per cent reduction, as do certain other business assets including a controlling interest in a trading company; there is also a 20 per cent reduction for minority interests in unquoted trading companies and agricultural land that is let out.

Finally, if you think you can avoid capital transfer tax just by leaving Britain, then you are mistaken. If you are deemed to be domiciled here the tax will apply to all your property wherever it is situated.

Chapter 6
HOUSING AND PROPERTY

From the beginning of the general move to home-ownership in the 1930s, buying a house has proved a marvellous investment — enabling both middle class and, more recently, working class home-owners to create capital. House prices have risen far faster than inflation as a whole, but the growth has not been evenly spread over the post-war years. What has happened in practice is that there has been a relatively short-lived boom, followed by a time of consolidation. But what creates the boom?

Perhaps the most notable rush to buy houses occurred in the early 1970s. It was helped by the fact that building society savers had not yet realized that the low inflation of the 1950s

84

and '60s had disappeared, and were still content with low interest rates, well below the rate of inflation. As a result, housebuyers had access to plenty of cheap money, and, as a matter of government policy, there was no limit to the amount you could borrow for house purchase with full tax relief, which made the money even cheaper.

It was an era of rising wages so the basic multiple on which a building society would lend produced large figures, and, almost for the first time, the working wife came into the picture. Advances in birth control methods meant she could plan her family so that if her earnings were needed to support the mortgage she could wait to have children.

However the house market overshot itself at that time and many people who bought in the early 1970s had to wait some years before they could say that their house had proved a good investment. At the end of the decade, though, prices once again began to rush ahead, outstripping inflation and leading people back to 'gazumping' (overriding an accepted offer for a house with a higher figure or other incentives such as cash payments, paying for removal and so on) and borrowing up to the hilt. Once again the key to the boom was that the mortgage rate, after tax relief, was well below inflation.

But will it continue? With lower inflation, and more sophisticated building society savers demanding their fair share, cheaper borrowing seems a thing of the past. The restriction of tax relief to £30,000 is already a restraining factor in the south of England. But the ultimate constraint on house prices has to be how much people can afford to pay, and this is dictated by their earnings. As long as earnings rise faster than inflation, house prices will go up.

For most people a house should not be viewed as an investment, never mind a speculation; it should be viewed as a home. How much of your income you wish to devote to your home must be a personal decision. Some people prefer a modest house and private education for their children; others put foreign travel before a spare bedroom; but the main reason for wanting a home of your own is that the alternatives are so much less attractive. The private rented sector is dwindling fast: apart from bedsitters and flatlet houses, there is very little hope of getting decent rented property. Even local authority housing is now being sold off to tenants, so the more attractive council housing will not be available for rent any longer.

Whether you like the idea of being a house-owner or not, you may soon have little choice. It is, therefore, important that you understand the economics of buying a house, since this is likely to be your most important financial transaction ever.

When you buy your first home or move to another property, the actual price is only the beginning. There are countless extra expenses that have to be taken into consideration and the total costs of moving can easily add up to £2,000 or £3,000 unless you are prepared to 'do it yourself'.

Estate agents

For a start there are your estate agent's fees, payable by the seller at about 1½ per cent of the purchase price, plus VAT. The agent's charge will depend on whether he gets sole agency (which is self-explanatory) or whether he has to share commission through a joint agency. Sole agency is probably a good idea if there is a reasonable demand in the market, but whatever agreement is made there should be some time limit; do not be afraid to shop around and establish precisely what an agent will do for his fees – the amount of free advertising you might get is one good example of how to drive a sensible bargain. Estate agents are covered by the 1979 Estate Agents Act which, amongst other things, requires them to operate separate client accounts and disclose any personal interest which they may have in the property appearing on their books.

'Property shops'   Although local estate agents always claim specialized knowledge and contacts within the area, it is increasingly possible to use the services of one of the computerized high street property shops. They usually charge a fixed amount of £50 or £100 regardless of the price of the house; for this, you may get a photo and description in the shop window and details of your property put on a computer, which can then be consulted by would-be buyers.

Reports of the service offered by these organizations vary; the better ones provide additional help to buyers through links with building societies, surveyors and solicitors. It is, however, advisable to be on your guard. £100 is a good deal of money to fork out for a few lines on a computer, especially as the fee is paid at the outset, unlike an estate agency, which will make no charge until your property has actually been sold.

Conveyancing

One area of costs which has led to increasing bitterness among home buyers has been the monopoly enjoyed by solicitors to undertake conveyancing. The argument that they overcharged for what was basically a very simple transaction eventually came to a head in 1983 when a Member of Parliament introduced a Private Member's Bill into the House of Commons which gained sufficient support from all parties for the government early in 1984 to decide it would formally legislate to reform the whole area.

Accordingly, legislation is to be introduced during the 1984–85 session of Parliament to allow suitably qualified non-solicitors, as well as banks and building societies, to undertake conveyancing work. At the same time there is to be an independent enquiry to examine the necessary safeguards and also the extent to which the general means of transferring a house can be improved.

In fact conveyancing charges by solicitors have not been regulated by the Law Society since 1973, and the Society has made available specially printed estimate forms to enable house-buyers to shop around. An independent survey showed wide variations in fees: from £218 to £370 for a house costing £20,000, and between £287 and £505 for one costing £35,000. Even so the general consensus seems to be that prices could have a good deal further to fall.

In the end the fee will depend on the complexity of the work, but the most important factor is probably the solicitor's liability if anything goes wrong. Conveyancers who have set up in recent years to by-pass the solicitors' monopoly, mostly offer some sort of insurance on title to the property, but until Parliament has safeguarded consumers, it is wise to proceed with great caution.

Stamp duty   Unlike agents' fees, stamp duty falls exclusively on the buyer, and the more expensive the house the more you have to pay. The 1984 Budget raised the threshold from £25,000 to £30,000 and at the same time the rate was reduced to 1 per cent. Lifting the threshold means that 9 out of 10 first-time buyers will no longer be liable for stamp duty. The main savings, however, come on properties costing more than £40,000, which previously attracted duty of 2 per cent.

The Land Registry

You will also incur costs in the form of fees payable to the Land Registry for recording and transferring the ownership (or title) of the property. Land Registry fees are charged on a scale related to the value of the property being transferred. There is also a charge for registering a mortgage. For a table of stamp duty and Land Registry fees, see the Appendix.

Building society fees

So far we have not referred to the role of the building society, and certainly for most buyers it is not even worth setting out to look for a house unless a building society or bank has indicated in advance its willingness in principle to put up the money. Although the different types of mortgage are dealt with later in this chapter, it is worth stressing that most societies charge differential rates of interest depending on how much you want to borrow, and unless you need under £20,000, you should check carefully in advance which societies offer the best deal in your price range.

Societies will also want to be certain that the property offers good security for the loan, and will order a survey and valuation. A few years ago it was common practice for the buyer not to be shown any of the reports prepared by the building society or bank. Competition has changed all that and now there is much more willingness to provide buyers with the supporting services they need, in many cases at a rate well below what they would have to pay privately. This applies to some legal costs as well as to surveyors and even estate agents; the day may not be all that far away when it will be possible to obtain a complete house buying service based on the building society branch office.

Fees charged by the building society or bank will, of course, be included within the mortgage itself and are not negotiable, but there is one question worth asking at the outset and that is whether there is any problem about paying off the mortgage early; there should not be but it is wise to check.

The structural survey As far as the survey is concerned, in broad terms you get what you pay for; it is a false economy to accept a superficial report on what is likely to prove the most important financial transaction of your life.

Incentives or special offers

You should consider very carefully the true value of any incentives that are attached to the sale of newly built homes. Builders with an eye to attracting first-time buyers may well offer mortgages subsidized in the first year, or carpets and curtains, special fittings and even a new car in the garage. Most of these things quickly lose their value and when the time comes to move on a few years later, there may be an unpleasant surprise in store when the suggested resale price turns out well below expectations, especially if there is a continuing supply of new homes in the area.

Removal costs

Finally there is the move itself. Expect to pay at least £150–£200, even if you are only moving five miles up the road; for longer distances and more substantial property the bill could easily come to £500 or even £1,000. It may be that your employer will be prepared to help, perhaps with a cheap loan. Again it pays to shop around, being careful always to check on the professional standing and competence of the removal firm concerned. Make sure they are properly covered by insurance; do not be tempted to pack breakables yourself as removal companies do not usually accept liability for damage done to items not packed by their men.

'Doing it yourself'

While stamp duty, Land Registry fees, and the building society's professional charges may be unavoidable, it is possible to save quite a lot of the costs of moving house if you are prepared to devote energy and time to it. You may well have had a crack at hiring your own van, getting friends and family to lend a hand with the back-breaking job of shifting furniture, but you could go a lot further than that.

You could, for example, be your own estate agent, putting a board outside your house with your own telephone number on display or inviting passers-by to 'enquire within'. Alternatively, you could advertise the property in the local or even national newspapers in the hope of finding a buyer and saving yourself £1,000 or more: you can always fall back on the local estate agent if your own efforts come to nothing. But do not be tempted to fix the price too low just to get a quick sale, or you will have lost with one hand more than you saved with the other.

Until Parliament has sorted out the whole area of conveyancing and has come up with a simplified process, there is a major cost saving for those prepared to do it themselves. With time and care it should be a straightforward clerical job, and although it is not to be recommended with leasehold property, there should be no problems with freehold registered houses. There is a whole range of useful books on this subject which we have listed under Further Reading in the Appendix.

Taking out a mortgage

Buying and selling are one-off transactions, but the cost of a mortgage is something you will have to live with for many years. So it is vitally important to understand the two distinct ways of borrowing money for house purchase, the repayment method and the endowment method.

The repayment method If you go for the repayment method, you deal only with the building society – paying interest and some of the capital back each month for the life of the loan. Assuming interest rates do not change, the monthly repayments remain static. In the early years when the outstanding loan is large, a larger proportion of the monthly instalment will be made up of interest payable on the loan, with only a little capital being paid off. As the years go by, the debt falls and so, therefore, does the interest, enabling you to pay off more and more of the capital.

Until 1983 gross repayments were made to the building society and tax relief on the interest was collected direct from the taxman, usually via your PAYE code. As a result you got far more tax relief in the early years, so the net cost of a repayment mortgage was much cheaper at the beginning. In these inflationary times, it is usually the first few years after buying a house that a mortgage is a financial burden, so the repayment basis had considerable advantages for first-time buyers and indeed anyone who was borrowing up to the hilt in order to buy a better, more expensive property.

MIRAS With the advent of *mortgage interest relief at source*, or MIRAS as it is known, the old 'gross profile' mortgage was abandoned by most building societies. Instead of the payments *before* tax relief being flattened out over the life of the loan, the *net* repayments were averaged out. This did away with the cheap beginning with extra tax relief that had made the repayment mortgage an 'easy-start' loan for many housebuyers. Complaints were made at the time, so some societies (and most banks) offered on request to reinstate the old-style gross profile mortgage. In practice, though, you are now most likely to find yourself paying a flat *net* repayment.

The endowment method The starting cost of the flat net

repayment mortgage was very similar to the low-cost endowment type and, since the spring of 1983, led to a boom in the selling of low-cost endowment mortgage policies. With an endowment-type mortgage you deal not only with a building society but also with an insurance company. From the building society you get an interest-only mortgage and, if the loan is under £30,000, basic-rate tax relief will be deducted at source. In parallel to this, you take out an endowment policy – which is essentially a savings scheme designed to mature in, say, 25 years' time, producing enough to repay the building society. Of course, in practice very few people stay in one house for 25 years; when you move, the building society helps itself to the proceeds of the sale of the house, not to the endowment policy which will not yet have matured.

The low-cost endowment   There used to be two types of endowment policy that could be attached to a mortgage: the 'non-profit' policy which was guaranteed to grow to exactly the right amount but which was basically very bad value for money in inflationary times; and the 'with-profits' policy, where you would have the opportunity to benefit from the investment success of the insurance managers but which was very expensive for most borrowers since when it matured it might easily be worth two or three times as much as the original loan.

Eventually a mixture of the two was invented which has become known as the 'low-cost endowment' and which performs better than the non-profit type since it does accumulate investment bonuses. Nowadays you might be offered a third choice: a unit-linked version with added risk but greater potential. Unlike the full 'with-profits' policy, the low-cost and unit-linked versions are designed to produce only a little more than you need in 25 years' time. Since the low-cost policy starts small, extra life cover is built in at the beginning to guarantee that the loan can be paid off if the borrower dies early.

The alternatives for most people are now a net constant repayment loan from a building society or a low-cost endowment mortgage, combining a building society and an insurance company. Between April 1983, when MIRAS came in, and March 1984 when tax relief on life assurance premiums was abolished for new policies, there was little to choose between them, and the building societies collected huge amounts of commission by encouraging borrowers to opt for the low-cost endowment.

But now the sums are different, so which should you go for? You might be surprised, bearing in mind the enormous publicity following the end of tax relief and indeed our own remarks earlier in the book, to learn that for the average first-time buyer, taking out a £20,000 mortgage over 25 years, the bill goes up from about £1,800 a year to £1,850. The reason for this apparently small increase is that the mortgage interest represents more than five times the cost of the insurance policy for a young couple, and tax relief was only 15 per cent of the premiums anyway.

It may therefore need only a minor adjustment either to premiums or to the guarantees demanded by building societies on the sum assured to keep low-cost endowments fully competitive. Remember both insurance companies and building societies have a strong vested interest in doing so.

Brokers, of course, make their living out of organizing insurance policies, and whenever mortgage finance is in short supply, they come into their own and will almost invariably recommend the endowment method. They also provide a useful service, if the property is old or you wish to borrow a large proportion of the purchase price, since they may have access to funds that you would otherwise be denied.

Disadvantages of the low-cost endowment The disadvantages of this route do not really become apparent until you try and 'trade up' a few years later. At that point you must refuse to surrender the first policy, particularly if it pre-dates the 1984 Budget. If you need to cover a larger mortgage, top it up with another policy. If you surrender the policy every time you move house you are simply wasting money, since you have to pay quite heavy commission, known as the *front end load*, to the insurance broker or salesman each time. If you are very pressed for cash, it will pay to ask around for the old-style 'gross profile' repayment mortgage, with the extra tax relief in the first few years.

Linking to a pension contract There is one relatively new idea which, for some people, can replace the endowment policy. If you are self-employed, you can link your mortgage to a self-employed pension contract, using your pension contributions as collateral for the loan. The advantage to you is that you get full tax relief on the savings element whereas endowment policies now have no relief at all. The advantage to the salesman is that he makes a lot more commission on a pension contract than on a low-cost endowment. For this reason, make sure you have studied the options carefully, and only go ahead if you expect to remain self-employed for years to come. If you stop a pension plan after a few years, there may be little left for you once the salesman has taken his commission. However, it is a welcome change for the self-employed to find themselves becoming attractive mortgage propositions. In the past they have been at a particular disadvantage in the mortgage queue, since building societies count as income only their taxable profits. All the doctoring of accounts that tends to go on among small businessmen and professional people works to their disadvantage when calculating what they can borrow. (See the following chapter under the section 'Pensions for the self-employed' to find out if you are eligible for this type of pension even if you are not technically self-employed.)

How much you can borrow

Building societies usually lend employed people 2½ times the main breadwinner's earnings; where they are lending to a couple, they may also take into account perhaps one times the smaller income. It is normal practice to lend up to 80 per cent of the value of the property, and that value will be the building society's or bank's valuation, rather than what you choose to pay for the house. If you need to go above that, you may be given a little more, particularly if you are a first-time buyer, but you can be asked to pay for an indemnity policy to insure the building society against the danger that you could default, leaving it with a property on which it cannot raise enough to cover the mortgage and all its costs.

First-time buyers

Over the years there have been all sorts of schemes to help first-time buyers, including the offer of 100 per cent mortgages, but they tend to date back to the era of fierce competition between banks and building societies and are unlikely to be repeated on any scale. In the normal way you must resign yourself to saving for the deposit over a year or so, and building up a track record with a lender. When mortgages are relatively plentiful, it is easy to forget what happens in a mortgage famine – then only regular savers over a long period will be offered loans. It will probably pay to save where you get some guarantee of a loan at the end.

In 1978 the government sponsored a first-time buyers' scheme on those lines, designed to give widescale help. The idea was that if you saved for 2 years (and put in at least £1,000 in the second year) you would get an interest-free loan of £600 with your basic mortgage as well as a gift of £110 towards costs. It has not proved much of an incentive, though, and only 1 buyer in 70 seems to have bothered with it.

Council house sales

When the Conservative government came into office in 1979 one of their main commitments in the field of housing was to allow council house tenants the right to buy their homes. This covered all 'secure tenants' who had lived in a council house for at least 3 years, with the exception of certain types of specialized accommodation for the disabled or for pensioners. The 1980 Housing Act which brought the legislation into force was bitterly opposed by the Labour Party and by Labour-controlled authorities, but it has none the less been widely taken up for one very good reason: the properties are available at a very substantial discount to their market value.

This discount starts at 33 per cent after 3 years' tenancy and rises by 1 per cent a year to a maximum of 50 per cent discount for tenants of 20 years' standing; there is also a right to a local authority mortgage and if you are unable to afford to buy immediately you can pay a modest, refundable deposit to keep an option open for up to 2 years at the original valuation. One important concession to buyers, incidentally, is that the stamp duty is calculated on the discounted price they pay for the house and not market value, so few actually pay it. The detailed rules and method of application will be found in leaflets available from your local authority housing department.

In the three years since the scheme came into effect (October 1980) 680,000 tenants have taken advantage of the right to buy and in 1983 the government proposed an extension of the scheme to help elderly tenants, but not those in sheltered or warden accommodation. At the same time they proposed that the

3-year qualifying period should be reduced to 2 years, starting with a 32 per cent discount and increasing by 1 per cent per year to a maximum of 60 per cent after 30 years. Providing the necessary bill goes through Parliament, it is expected to become law by late summer 1984.

Buying the freehold of a leased property
Another less well-publicized right to buy is available to people who own a leasehold property and who wish to buy the freehold. It must, incidentally, be a house, not a flat. There are a number of qualifications, which cover the rateable value, the level of ground rent and the duration of the lease, which must have been granted for more than 21 years. The main difficulty may be in establishing a fair price, given that the leaseholder has the right to occupy the property for the rest of the lease and the right to extend the lease when it runs out. With legal help, some transactions may be satisfactorily completed at a cost of a few hundred pounds; others may take years of wrangling and may in any case turn out to be far too expensive to contemplate.

Home improvements
Few owners find any new home totally to their liking; once you have got over the initial hurdle of buying the property, you may well decide to improve it. Whether it is a question of 'do it yourself', double-glazing, getting a new damp course put in, or adding a full-scale architect-designed extension, home improvements are very big business, although the imposition of 15 per cent VAT on alterations may give the market a setback. Unfortunately people's inclination to spend money on their homes has spawned a huge number of unscrupulous salesmen and builders offering over-priced and shoddy workmanship; they then either disappear without trace or go bankrupt, leaving the householder without any redress, and the new VAT rules will not help.

Despite considerable government involvement through the range of improvement grants which are available from local authorities, there is relatively little consumer protection other than that included within the general law. The Office of Fair Trading gets a continual stream of complaints about the unfair contracts and worthless guarantees that abound within an industry where trade associations often have very little more real substance than a piece of elaborately headed notepaper.

Local authority grants Anyone considering having work done to improve his or her home, or to bring an older property up to a decent standard, should find out first how much money can be obtained from the local authority. Grants fall broadly into two categories – those which are mandatory, covering the provision of essential services such as inside lavatories, kitchens, heating and running water; and those which are discretionary, covering the general cost of repairs, improvements and conversions.

There is also a separate grant towards putting in proper roof insulation, and the rule that used to exclude any home with even the barest minimum layer of existing insulation has now been relaxed, so that in future you will be allowed to put in additional insulation up to a maximum of 101 mm (4 ins), provided that there are not more than 25 mm (1 in) of existing insulation in the loft. The date when this comes into effect has not yet been fixed, but it will be some time during 1984. There is no change in the amount of the grant: two thirds of the cost of putting the insulation in, or nine tenths if you are disabled or a pensioner.

It is one thing to qualify for the mandatory or discretionary grants; it is another to get your hands on the money. Because the schemes have turned out to be so popular, long delays have built up in certain areas despite the fact that funds allocated by central government rose from under £100 million in 1978 to over £500 million in 1983, during which year the government announced cutbacks so that maximum grants from 1 April 1984 are only 75 per cent instead of 90 per cent of eligible expenditure. The attitude of certain councils may also be affected by their political allegiance, and discretionary grants give councils just that discretion, against which there is no appeal.

Top-up loans Apart from official help, however, it is quite likely that the building society or bank which originally gave you a mortgage will be prepared to help with a top-up loan for home improvements. Their willingness may be governed by the general demand for new mortgages but most societies keep a separate pool of money for this purpose, though you would be well advised to check the precise terms. Some societies charge a half per cent or 1 per cent extra if the new loan takes your total borrowings over a particular threshold. Others need to know precisely what the money is being used for and will naturally charge considerably more to finance a swimming pool than a new roof.

Getting the work done   You will obviously have a very good idea of what the work is going to cost when you apply for a loan, and you should also have cleared any necessary planning permission. But the decision as to who does the job is an individual one. For smaller jobs, recommendations by friends or neighbours who can show evidence of work well done may be the best solution, while paying for proper supervision by an architect is essential for substantial or complex contracts. It is vital to be quite clear at what point you will be expected to part with any money, and staged payments should be linked to satisfactory completion of agreed targets.

In the last year or so the professional bodies, such as the RIBA (The Royal Institute of British Architects) and RICS (The Royal Institution of Chartered Surveyors) have become increasingly concerned about standards and their own liability in the event of things going wrong. Professional indemnity insurance is the main public safeguard; as far as the building trade is concerned, it is now possible to guarantee contract completion through a bonded builder scheme. This ensures not only that the work will be completed if the original firm goes bust, but also that it will be done with the proper materials and to the specified standards. It remains to be seen, however, whether the pressure of public opinion and the willingness to deal only with registered firms will eventually put the cowboys out of business.

Legal expenses insurance   A further safeguard worth considering is to take out legal expenses insurance, which will cover your costs in the event of a dispute. This type of cover can be provided either separately by one of the specialist insurers or as an extension to general household cover. Any insurance broker will be able to advise.

Housing and the elderly

Owning your own property is generally seen as an asset, yet to many elderly people houses are a liability as the cost of maintenance and repairs weighs more and more heavily on their limited resources. Some building societies will now agree to make an *interest only loan*, which is, of course, tax allowable, for the purpose of improving a property. As the name suggests, an interest only loan is one on which you pay only the interest, without having to repay part of the capital by instalments at the same time. The capital sum is usually repaid from the proceeds of selling the house, which may be on your death.

The distinction between an improvement and a repair is not easy to define, but societies will usually offer help and advice to the elderly, especially if they have been savers over a long period of time.

This does not alter the fact that a home is a non-income producing asset and the cost of paying rates, electricity, gas and telephone, quite apart from general maintenance and repairs, increases year by year. When the children have left to set up homes of their own and a couple have reached retirement age with the inevitable drop in income, they may find it increasingly hard to make ends meet.

For many people the solution is to trade down, to buy a smaller house or flat in a more convenient area with lower outgoings. This will enable them to realize some of the capital gain that has built up over the years in their original home, and to invest it to produce extra income. Others are reluctant to pull up their roots, to exchange a familiar environment for something which they may not like or which may prove to have hidden disadvantages. This may not be such a problem for those with reasonable occupational pensions as well as state ones (which will be increased over time) as it is for those older pensioners who may have nothing but the state on which to rely. The latter may be attracted to what is called a *home income plan* or *mortgage annuity scheme*.

The home income plan   A home income plan involves taking out a mortgage on your home and then using the proceeds to buy an annuity. Part of the annuity goes to pay off the mortgage interest and the balance is available to boost your income. Since annuities are more lightly taxed than other types of investment income, because part of the money is regarded as a return of capital, those who qualify can improve their living standards without the expense and upset of having to move.

The main difficulty is age. To obtain a sufficiently attractive annuity you really need to be at least 70 years old; married couples will need a combined age of 150, with the wife at least 73. There are other considerations: for example, one of the big companies involved does not allow you to borrow more than 80 per cent of the value of the house, while another limits it to 65 per cent, and there is a £30,000 top limit on loans. However, you do not lose the ownership of the property, and, if at a later date you find the value has risen substantially, then you can always go back for a top-up. The loan itself will be paid off at your death when the property can be sold.

The net gain of a home income plan varies depending on age and the size of the loan, and it is important to take account of any welfare benefits that may be at risk, especially supplementary pension or help with the rates; that apart, a house worth £35,000 could produce extra income of about £1,500 a year to a single person in his or her early seventies.

Although a great many people are attracted by the idea in principle, relatively few take it up in practice. In any event it is essential to take proper financial and legal advice first to make sure you are not involving yourself in a so-called *reversionary scheme*. This involves actually selling your home to a company (a reversion). Although you retain the right to live in it for the rest of your life, to take account of this the cash sum you are paid will be well below the property's market value and you may be offered as little as 40 per cent or 50 per cent. As house prices continue to rise and inflation reduces the value of the extra income you may have secured by the reversionary scheme, it could turn out to have been a disastrous mistake in 5 or 10 years' time.

Buying a home for a relative   If you buy a home for an elderly relative, there can be considerable tax saving. The relative must be considered to be a dependant by the taxman; or it could be your widowed, divorced or separated mother – irrespective of her state of health. If you have taken out a loan to buy the house or flat, you can claim mortgage interest tax relief as long as the person concerned lives in the property rent-free. The loan has to be taken into account in fixing your top limit for tax relief at £30,000 but any growth in the value of the property is also totally free of capital gains tax on sale. Helping someone in the family to buy property in old age could prove a sensible investment in its own right, as long as you can afford to tie money up (and even borrow) for some years without charging any rent.

Housing benefits   Another way to help less well-off members of the family is to explore some of the welfare benefits they may be entitled to. Both Age Concern and the Child Poverty Action Group publish useful books and pamphlets on both means-tested and statutory benefits; these are listed under Further Reading in the Appendix.

Until the spring of 1983, there were two distinct sources of help for those in hardship with housing costs. First, there were *rent and rate rebates* and *rent allowances* (rebates for private sector tenants). These were administered by the local author-ity and based on the concept of the *needs allowance* — a fictional amount of money you are supposed to need to live on. If your income exactly matched the needs allowance, you would get 60 per cent of your rent and rates rebated. If your income went above this needs allowance, the rebate was tapered off, whereas if your income was below it you would get more. Secondly, and quite separately, there was the hous-ing component of the supplementary benefit provided by the Department of Health and Social Security. The key measure was the *scale rate*; again your contribution was based on where your income fell in relation to it. The difficulty for appli-cants was to know which of these benefits to apply for, with their entirely different rules, so in an attempt at reform the two benefits were merged.

The exercise was supposed to be achieved at no overall loss but, in fact, all previous beneficiaries lost out with the one exception of pensioners on supplementary benefit. There have since been further reductions in benefits, again attacking the better-off applicant through the so-called 'tapers' — that is the rate at which benefit tails off for those at the top end of the income scale. This, of course, intensifies the poverty trap, since a small increase in the family's income can result not only in national insurance and tax increases but in a sudden loss of benefit. There have been proposed changes but the position is very unclear at present, so ask your local authority housing officer to work out the sums for you.

If in doubt, get the literature from the local authority and try the sums out. SHAC also produces excellent leaflets on the sub-ject, which are listed under Further Reading (Housing and Social Security) in the Appendix. All too often benefits are not claimed because people will not submit themselves to the prying that is entailed in a means test. For unemployed home-owners whose savings have run below £3,000, exploring the possibility of the unified housing benefit is critical, because it can pay mortgage interest until another job can be found and so remove the fear of eviction.

If you do lose your job and you have a mortgage to pay off, your first port of call must be to the building society or bank. As long as they are kept fully in the picture, they can prove extremely helpful and considerate by putting you, for example, on interest only payments for a time.

Letting a property

Those who have difficulty in finding a job may have to think of moving to another area, or even going abroad to look for work. It is possible to let your home for a time without losing any of the tax advantages of home ownership – mortgage interest relief and capital gains tax exemption will continue for several years, as we point out in Chapter 4. But you should certainly consult a solicitor before installing tenants in your home – ask about special tenancy arrangements to ensure repossession of your property at the end of the tenancy. You should also draw up an inventory of your possessions to prevent any argument about breakages, and establish quite clearly at the outset just who is to pay the rates, heating and lighting bills.

If you go overseas and leave a local estate agent to manage the property on your behalf, he is obliged to deduct basic-rate tax from the rent, but you may be able to reclaim some of this, depending on your other British income, allowances and charges. You can also offset some of the expenses of letting against tax – wear and tear, replacement, postage, even inspection visits.

Lodgers   There used to be a snag for anyone who let out part of a home to lodgers when it came to capital gains tax. The rules have now been relaxed so that CGT rarely applies. To calculate your liability, take the period during which the lodgers have been in residence and the proportion of the house they occupy in relation to the whole period of your own occupation. For example, if you have lived in the house for 20 years, but for the last 4 years half the house has been let out to tenants, 4 out of 20 is a fifth, or 20 per cent. Halve that and you get 10 per cent. In the old days 10 per cent of the gain in the house's value would have been liable to CGT, but now, unless that gain is over £10,000, it will be ignored. If you have had tenants for longer, their share of the gain might reach £10,000, but even then everyone is allowed £5,300 of gain before tax is payable, so few people need to worry.

Whether or not income from tenants counts as earned or investment income depends on the services that you provide, and, with the investment income surcharge now scrapped, it may anyway be academic for most landlords. If it is counted as earned income, however, it may be allowed for business retirement relief when sold by someone of 65 or over.

Holiday lets   One substantial concession which the government brought in helps people with furnished holiday lettings. Previously some had been able to treat these as a business, while others were obliged to have the rents treated as investment income. The new rules introduced in the 1984 Budget (but which have been backdated to April 1982) allow anyone with holiday accommodation to treat the income as earned; it can accrue either to husband or wife, and if the property is sold you will be allowed to defer any charge to capital gains tax provided that you buy another property. You may also qualify for business retirement relief, which can now be as much as £100,000.

The main qualifications are that the accommodation must be let on a commercial basis with a view to making profits; it must be available to the public for at least 180 days during the season, from April to October; and you must have paying tenants for at least 90 days during this period, though none of them must occupy the accommodation for more than 30 days at a time. As the season actually runs for 214 days, the owner will be able to take a summer holiday in the property for a month during this period and to occupy the premises or have a long letting during the winter months.

There is no doubt that the new rules will benefit a great many people, though it remains to be seen how they work out in practice. The usual trading expenses will be allowable, including wear and tear allowances, and it appears that those who have satisfied the rules prior to 1982 (even though they were not in existence) will be able to claim both capital gains tax roll-over relief and business retirement relief for those previous years. If in future the conditions are not met in any single year, the reliefs will be scaled back, but consistently missing them will almost certainly mean the Revenue questioning your motives and disallowing your claim.

Chapter 7
YOU AND YOUR PENSION

By tomorrow
these will be the
good old days...

A pension is simply part of your pay given to you when you retire, instead of while you are working. For this reason you pay no tax during your working life on the earnings you sacrifice by way of contributions; when you collect your pension you are taxed on the money as earned income, because it is quite simply pay which you have chosen to defer until you are older. In practice, most people have little or no say in the matter. Their employers decide how good their pension ought to be and how much both employer and employee need to set aside as a percentage of pay to achieve it. Indeed, many people have no clear idea of what they would get at retirement, and are often dumbfounded when they find out what happens to their pensions if they decide on early retirement.

It is sensible to find out how to evaluate your own pension rights if they come as part of the job, and how you can supplement them if they are less than you would have chosen to provide yourself. You should also know what questions to ask if you plan to leave early and what the position would be for your dependants if you die before or after retirement. Even so the state pension is still the basis of security in retirement for most people. How much is it worth and how will the improved 'earnings related' benefits work out in practice as the scheme gets under way?

The self-employed have no pension entitlements to fall back on at all unless they make their own provision, so it is worth discovering how to set about it and what the tax rules are. Some people reach retirement with totally inadequate pensions, yet it is still possible to buy an income for life through a purchased life annuity. Is it then a sensible investment? These are some of the questions this chapter seeks to answer.

Pension schemes for the employed

For people in regular employment, there are two possibilities. You may be contracted in to the *state earnings related scheme*, which means your contributions go towards giving you extra state benefits at retirement. This is on top of the flat-rate national insurance contributions all employees have to pay for the basic state pension. Your employer, however, may have chosen to contract out of the extra state benefits on your behalf and substitute an *occupational scheme* in its place. The occupational scheme must be better than the state provisions or the employer will not be allowed to contract out. There is in fact a third possibility, where you remain contracted in to the state scheme but have some additional benefits on top. This is known in the trade as 'living-on-top' and we will come back to it after explaining occupational and state earnings related benefits.

Private occupational schemes

If your employer runs an occupational scheme, you will be given a booklet about your pension which gives you the basic outline and defines the expressions used. To understand it, you need a little background to pension thinking. Nowadays most schemes are known as *final salary schemes*, because your benefits at retirement are based on a certain proportion of your final salary for each year of service with the company. Perhaps the most common occupational pension is known as a *sixtieths scheme*, where you get $\frac{1}{60}$ of pay for each year of service. If you have worked for 40 years with one employer, you would get the maximum pension of $\frac{40}{60}$, which is two thirds of your pay. If you have only worked 20 years, you would get $\frac{20}{60}$ or one third, and so on.

For pension purposes, 'pay' is not always 'final salary'. At best it will be earnings in the last 12 months before you retire, but often it is the average annual pay over the last 3 years, which can prove quite a lot less if there have been good pay rises in the last year or so of your working life. You may find your pension booklet uses the term 'pensionable salary' rather than final salary. This is because many schemes include a *national insurance abatement*, based on the theory that, since at best you need only two thirds of your pay in retirement, you can deduct the basic state retirement pension to save double counting.

These schemes take one and a half times the state pension off your final salary to come up with 'pensionable salary'. Multiply that by two thirds and you will see that at most they claw back a single pension, with shorter-serving employees having a scaled-down loss. The national insurance abatement tends to work out at roughly £2,500 off the final salary (or average pay over the last 3 years), so for lower-paid workers it makes a big difference to the proportion of pay they get as pension.

Calculating your pension   Of course, you do not know what you will be earning when you retire, or what your state pension will be, so the sensible thing to do is to work out all the figures on today's pay and at least find out on what proportion of pay your pension is likely to be based. It gives you a clear idea of what your pension might mean in today's money and that, after all, is the only thing most of us can understand. A word of warning though. Many good pension schemes only go back to the 1970s. You could find that your service for the last few years counts as $\frac{1}{60}$ for each year, but before that it might be as little as $\frac{1}{80}$, $\frac{1}{120}$ or even, in some cases, nothing. If in doubt, ask the pension department what your pensionable service will be and how many sixtieths or eightieths you will get. They have it all on record, and most pension people are delighted to help when someone takes an interest in their subject.

Indexation and growth   Having established what proportion of today's pay you are likely to get when you retire, the next questions are all about the quality of the pension and, most important of all, how fast it will grow. Indexation is, of course, the dream; a pension that rises in line with prices is worth about 80 per cent more than a flat pension. However, most pensions offer far less. If a guarantee of annual increases is built in, it might be at 3 per cent per annum or possibly 5 per cent, but anything over that is only payable if the funds are well managed. Check with the pensions department because, although there may be no guarantees, there may be a good history of one-off increases.

Widows' rights   Women outlive men by about 5 to 1 so widows' rights are worth checking. Half, or even two thirds, of a husband's pension might be built in to a widow's pension. There is often a guarantee that it will be paid in full for the first 5 years of retirement whether the husband survives or not. The best schemes now treat widowers the same as widows.

Lump-sum payments   Finally, you may have a right to opt for a tax-free lump sum, known as *commutation*, as part of the pension at retirement. The best schemes allow you to take a proportion of your pension in this way. It can be up to one and a half year's pay as a lump sum, if you have done more than 20 years' service. Whether or not to commute is one of the major financial decisions of life for many people. You will need to ask how much pension you give up for how much cash. With that sort of lump sum, you can almost certainly do better in the first year or so than from a pension, by investing the money, even in a building society. As commutation must improve your family's security, the temptation is to take the cash.

If there is a history of decent increases in the pension, however, you might find replacing the lost pension from your lump sum will become increasingly difficult as the years go on. How soon would you have been better off to have stuck with the pension? The simple calculation is to set out two columns; in the first, put the annual investment income you could get on the lump sum, for example, by putting the money into a building society. In the other column, put the after-tax pension you are sacrificing each year, but increase it year by year at some realistic rate. Work out how old you would be at the point when the two columns are equal; that is the age when opting for a pension would begin to pay off, although actually you would have to live a few years after that to make up for the shortfall early in retirement. Commuting does pay for most people, but the truth is that the offer of a lump sum is usually irresistible, whatever the figures tell you.

Some schemes give you no choice on the question of a lump sum; it is dished out to you automatically. This is much more common in the public sector; with the civil service pension, for example, you get $1/80$ of pay for each year of service, plus three years' pension in a tax-free lump sum. It works out like a sixtieth scheme, but with automatic commutation.

After 40 years on a sixtieth scheme, you get two thirds of pay: if you are earning £12,000 a year, that means a pension of £8,000, of which you can sacrifice up to a quarter for a tax-free lump sum. As a general guideline, each £1 of pension could result in £9 of cash, so you could give up £2,000 a year of pension and receive £18,000 tax-free, and be left with £6,000 a year of pension.

Now see what happens with the civil service eightieth scheme for the same salary after 40 years. You will get $40/80$ (or one half) of £12,000, so your pension will be £6,000 per annum, and you have three years' pension as a tax-free lump sum of £18,000. Thus you end up with exactly the same as if you were in the private sector and had chosen to commute.

Changing jobs   Apart from inflation-proofing, the main difference between the private and public sectors comes when moving from one job to another. In the public sector, your years with one department normally count as years with the next: although you may have moved from job to job, for pension purposes your service is continuous.

It is a very different matter in the private sector. Let us say you worked between the ages of 35 and 45 for Company A and leave earning £12,000. Your pension entitlement is $10/60$ times £12,000 – or £2,000 a year. But that is only payable from the age of 65 and may well be frozen in the meantime. If you go to Company B and ask to transfer your pension, will you get 10 additional years? No, because Company B will say by the time you come to retire at 65, they calculate you will be earning close on £100,000. Now $10/60$ of that would mean £16,000 a year, whereas Company A are only going to contribute enough, by way of transfer value, to buy £2,000 (their frozen pension). Thus

Company B will say they cannot give you 10 years for your transfer, only just under 2.

Many people have now caught on to this appalling snag in private sector schemes and realize that, all too often, they are living in a fool's paradise. Because they are on a good pension scheme, they may think their old age is taken care of. Then they find that with broken service, often through no fault of their own, the pension is, in fact, quite poor. At first the response of the pension industry was to say, 'Tough luck; you went off to better yourself, so why should your ex-employer be expected to pay up?' But now the government has intervened and legislation is to be brought in to force employers to increase prospective pensions for their ex-employees until such time as the pension can be drawn. It will not apply to old jobs, nor even to past service, but it should go some way to overcome the fundamental disadvantages inherent in occupational schemes for mobile workers.

'Money purchase' or 'portable' pension schemes

Another solution has been put forward which effectively winds the clock back. The whole idea of sixtieth and suchlike schemes is to link starting pensions to final salaries, considered a critical advantage in times of high inflation. As inflation has stabilized at around 5 per cent, people are now talking of going back to the old idea of *money purchase*. This simply says that each year your and your employers' contributions will be put into a fund with your name on it. When you retire, you will collect a little parcel from each year of your working life, with all the interest and growth attaching to it. This way it is irrelevant whether you have worked for one employer or twenty.

It sounds the perfect solution, so why does it in fact not overcome all our difficulties? With a final salary scheme, the employers' contributions for younger workers are very small because the contributions have many years to grow before being needed, whereas people fondly imagine that a money purchase scheme would put an equally large contribution into the fund for each year of service. However, if this did happen, it would push up the cost of pensions out of all recognition. These so-called 'portable pensions' are, however, useful for people who work for small companies, where setting up a full-blown final salary scheme would be administratively wasteful.

Portable pensions are also often used for those people who are *living-on-top* of the state scheme. Where basic security in retirement comes from being contracted in to the state scheme, additional rights are bought year by year, often depending on the profitability of a small company. The amount payable each year for each member of staff, or director, is then simply earmarked for his or her personal use at retirement.

Additional voluntary contributions

One use of a money purchase pension which is becoming increasingly available is an AVC or *additional voluntary contributions scheme*. This is set up by the employer and usually run by an insurance company or even a building society; employees may volunteer to set aside the difference between their compulsory contributions to the main scheme and 15 per cent of their pay to buy extra pension rights. Their contributions will be fully tax-deductible and will be invested in a tax-free fund until retirement, when they will be paid out either as a pension, or in some cases as a tax-free lump sum. Occasionally AVC plans are set up to give added years on top of the main pension, but this is more common in the public sector where some AVC schemes are also index-linked.

AVC schemes are highly tax-efficient for those who are concerned about a pension shortfall in retirement, but the take-up tends to be small. It is reckoned that some 83 per cent of workers could join an AVC plan of some sort, but only 7 per cent actually do. If saving for your old age is your most important need, however, look carefully at AVCs and ask for an example to be worked out for you, particularly if you are a high-rate taxpayer. Most employers put these schemes in to please their staff and then tend to be disappointed at the take-up rate, so your interest would be welcomed.

State pensions

For those who remain contracted in, the *additional component* of the state pension scheme is intended to supplement the flat-rate benefit. After World War II a fundamental mistake was made in designing the Welfare State. It was decided that national insurance contributions should be the same for everyone, irrespective of earnings. The contribution level therefore had to be fixed at what every employee could afford, and so it was effectively linked to an agricultural labourer's wage. As a result, the state retirement pension was also tied to the needs of a low-paid worker, and compared to many other countries the British state pension is very small in relation to average earnings.

In 1961, it was boosted by an earnings-related ('graduated') pension but that did not prove adequate, so, after years of debate, in 1977 the concept of 'contracting in or out' was brought in. The additional component for the state scheme has set the pace for a fundamental improvement in pensions, and employers could only contract out if they were prepared to better it. So, for those left simply with the state, what does the additional component provide?

It does not come fully to fruition until 1998 — with the equivalent of $\frac{1}{80}$ of pay for a maximum of 20 years' service. At best you get a quarter of your pay on top of the flat-rate scheme. It may not sound much compared with the half and two thirds of pay promised under many occupational schemes but it has one great advantage. If you move jobs, those state eightieths are not frozen but effectively index-linked, and as a result the ultimate pension will be something you can really bank on. No contracted-out scheme can fall below this level, known as the *guaranteed minimum pension*, and this GMP is escalated in retirement not by the employer but by the state.

The GMP covers earnings up to some £13,000 a year and even with contracted-out schemes is central to transfer values, since these essential requirements must be met and presented at every job change, as well as at retirement. However, higher-paid staff would be ill-served by a contracted-in scheme, unless they were 'living-on-top'.

State pensions for married women   There are special rules for married women when it comes to the flat state pension. Just because a married woman has not paid national insurance contributions for many years, it does not mean she will not be able to draw some flat-rate state pension in her own right. The basic rule is that she must have contributed for a quarter of her working life — usually 11 out of 44 qualifying years, but it may be less for people in work before 1948.

The confusion that has arisen hinges on the change in the rules in 1979. Those married women who reached the age of

60 before 6 April had to meet an additional qualification: the *half test*. This meant that they had to have paid full-rate contributions for at least half the number of years between getting married and reaching the age of 60. So a typical wartime bride, born in 1918, married in 1940, perhaps working until 1944 before starting a family, might have clocked up 7 years of contributions; she might then have done perhaps another 10 years' full-time work after bringing up her family. Her total contributions of 17 years, however, would have fallen just short of half the 38 years of her married life, so no pension.

But consider the same woman born a few years later, retiring perhaps in 1982, and so avoiding the half test. In this case, her contribution record will be sufficient to earn her a pension, though it must be stressed that the contributions must have been paid at the full rate and not the reduced rate for which married women were able to opt up until 1979.

All this is of little consequence if the woman is more than 5 years younger than her husband, because if that is the case, at age 65 he may well draw a larger pension for his wife as a dependant on his contributions than she has in her own right. The only advantage then is that the part attributable to his wife's earnings will be tax-free under the married women's earnings allowance.

With the move to equality, all those old rules have now been scrapped. Women can no longer opt out of the flat-rate pension and their increasing importance as breadwinners is reflected in the new contribution rules. They pay the same as men, except when they are at home looking after children – when they will be given credits for home responsibility – and in years to come, the working wife will retire with her pension entitlement to supplement her husband's rights from his job. Gone will be the idea that it is the husband who provides the income both in work and in retirement.

Pensions for the self-employed

As pension provisions improved for employees, it became increasingly obvious that, unless steps were taken, the new poor would be the self-employed in retirement. The additional component of the state scheme does not apply to them and they are left to pay not only for their own share of their pension but in effect the employer's contributions as well. To encourage the self-employed to match the employed in acquiring security for their old age, the government has relaxed the rules about tax relief on what are known as *self-employed deferred annuities*, or SEDAs for short. Again the principle stands that pension contributions are simply deferred pay so, up to a point, should escape tax at the time and be taxed as earnings when paid back in the form of a pension.

The limits have been raised now to allow anyone under the age of 51 to pay in 17½ per cent of earnings, without the cut-off point for higher earnings which applied up to 1980. At age 50, the percentage goes up to 20 per cent. If you have left it very late, and like many self-employed people are still having to work in your late sixties or early seventies, you can contribute up to 29 per cent of pay with full tax relief up till your 75th brithday. The case for making self-employed contributions on a SEDA towards the end of your career is quite compelling, and, since part of your entitlement can promptly be drawn out again as a tax-free lump sum, the residual pension costs very little.

Working wives Another group of people who should look closely at self-employed pensions are working wives approaching retirement. When pensions are paid, they are taxed as earned income; pension from a wife's own contributions counts as her own, so it can be offset against her wife's earned income relief, making it tax-free up to £2,005 or so a year. By using the wife's right to make pension contributions, a couple can convert any available savings into pension contributions and soon take it back, after full tax relief, as part tax-free lump sum and part tax-free income.

Although these schemes tend to be called *self-employed pensions* that is only a shorthand expression for pensions available to anyone who, for any reason, is precluded from being in a company scheme. They can be used by people with a second non-pensionable source of income, by those who are too old to join a company scheme, or whose employers are too small to have set up a scheme themselves.

Tax relief on SEDA The main users of a SEDA will, of course, be the self-employed. A significant concession a few years back has increased the flow of business into SEDAs by allowing people up to 6 years to make back contributions and still be granted tax relief. All too often self-employed people get their finances in a mess; their tax may not have been sorted out for several years back or their accounts agreed. When they do finally get themselves organized, however, they are now allowed to make up for lost time by going back to former years and offsetting pension contributions against the present tax liability.

It may, however, still leave a problem of cash flow. It is easy enough to get the tax relief if you have the money for the contributions. Now even that problem can be eased because of a new development to lend part of your pension back to you for use in your business or profession, or even to pay for school fees or a second home. As long as you pay a commercial rate of interest on the loan there are few questions asked. Indeed, a market is now developing in *loan back mortgages*, based on the idea that, at worst, the loan will be repaid from the tax-free lump-sum entitlement at retirement. As the loan has to be repaid anyway, it seems sensible to take advantage of full tax relief on pension contributions.

Another major advantage of a SEDA as a way of saving is that you can get tax relief on a single year's contributions without long-term commitments to the future. This is designed to help those with variable profits. The right to full tax relief on single premiums tends not to be over-emphasized as insurance brokers make vastly more commission out of getting you to sign on the dotted line for regular contributions up to retirement than for a mere one-off payment.

Taking advice   Nonetheless, it does pay to consult a broker who can discuss such aspects as the difference between unit-linked contracts and more conventional with-profits plans, and who can take you through the track records of the many insurance companies now competing for your business. At retirement date, you can ask for your pension rights to be uplifted to a different insurance company where you might get better value for regular monthly payments for life. This is known as exercising your right to the *open-market option* – another reason for enlisting the help of a professional adviser.

Brokers can also help the self-employed with a whole range of other policies available to put them into a comparable position to those in employment, for example, permanent health insurance (PHI) to provide income during prolonged disability; extra basic protection-only insurance; and inexpensive accident cover. These are all described in more detail in Chapter 8.

Death-in-service provisions

Before buying too much life insurance of their own, employed people should ask what happens under their pension scheme in the event of early death. The protection side of the insurance from your job will be broken down into three or four parts. There may be medical cover to pay for private hospitalization and specialists; permanent health cover might provide you with an income of up to three-quarters of your pay to normal retirement date minus state benefits (or sometimes two thirds or half) — check whether it increases to keep pace, at least to some extent, with inflation. Then there may be one or two benefits for early death, one a pension for a surviving spouse and the other a lump sum.

The maximum lump-sum death-in-service benefit is normally equal to 4 years' pay. Somewhere between 2 and 4 years is quite common these days with relatively benevolent employers, so it is as well to ask exactly what, if anything, your family would get on your death by way of a lump sum. If you are in a contracted-out scheme, there is almost certain to be a payment from the pension itself, which is often described in a complicated formula which you will need to spend a quarter of an hour or so disentangling.

Sometimes it is 'half prospective pension', so work out how long you have to serve to the normal retirement date and thus how many sixtieths or eightieths or whatever you would get. Translate that back into a percentage of your pay – a sum you will have to do anyway to work out your own pension. Then halve your pension to see what your widow would get if you die any time between now and retirement date. Check what sort of escalation there is for a widow's pension in payment and find out if there is anything for dependent children until their education is complete. You may find that there is a limit to 'prospective pensions' – perhaps a cut-off point, such as a minimum of 25 years unless actual service is greater.

Only when you can see just what benefits are available to you from your employer should you consider paying for extra protection. Remember, if you lost your job you might lose a lot more of your security than simply your salary. Some schemes contain the right to take out life cover to replace company death-in-service plans if you do so immediately on leaving. Check the small print here too, for there is often a restriction on the type of cover you can take out and you will be asked to pay normal rates. Usually the only advantage is for those who have to leave through ill health, as these continuing options do not require medical evidence.

Do not underestimate the advantages a good job can provide. When you have calculated what your ultimate pension would be as a proportion of pay, do this simple sum: first calculate your pension in terms of today's pay. Then double that figure for every 10 years between now and when you retire. That would not be far from your starting pension at retirement. To see what it would cost you to provide, if you were not in the scheme, multiply that annual figure by 7 if there is no increase in the pension; multiply it by 13 if it is fully index-linked. With lower guarantees go for something between the two – say for 5 per cent escalation, multiply by 10 and so on. Throw in a couple of years of your pension to put a lump-sum value on the continuing widow's rights and you will not be far off.

As an example in concrete figures, if today's pay is £8,000 at age 45, a 50 per cent pension at retirement age of 65 will be £4,000 per annum, also in today's figures. If the pension is inflation-adjusted over 20 years, it will be £16,000 per annum. The cost of this times 7 is £112,000; times 13 is £208,000. Widow's rights would cost £32,000. The total value of your pension would therefore be £144,000 (non-indexed) or £240,000 (indexed). Remember, though, it only comes to you as long as you stick the course – a sobering thought, if you are getting restless in your present job.

Chapter 8
INSURANCE FOR PROTECTION

Doctor – I keep getting these pains in my wallet...

If you know for certain that some expense is going to crop up, and you have enough money, you will set aside some savings to cover it. If you are not so certain about future expenses, it is difficult to know what to do. If you were the only person in the world, you would just have to take the risk; you could not afford to set money aside to cover every eventuality. You would simply have to hope that the fire, the premature death, the motor accident or whatever, would not happen to you.

With insurance, however, if you get enough people to band together, they can each pay a small contribution into a fund so that the unlucky man, woman or indeed family to suffer the loss will collect the proceeds. For example, put a thousand people into a hall and tell them that one of them will die some time during the next 12 months. Who will it be? We do not know; they are all young, fit and healthy. But if each of them pays £1 a week into a pool, when that one man or woman dies, his or her family will get £50,000. That in its most simple form is insurance. Do the same for burglary, fire, motor accidents and so on, and the average family man could spend a hundred or so pounds a year to protect himself and his family against a whole variety of financial disasters, all of which he hopes he will not suffer. The greatest hope you have in paying out for protection-only insurance is that the premiums will, with hindsight, prove to have been money down the drain.

This chapter is not about life insurance for savings, which was covered in Chapter 2 and is quite different. It is the mere historical accident of life assurance tax relief that allowed the British to use life policies for savings. The insurance in this chapter is pure protection, sometimes called insurance and sometimes assurance.

The confusion in these terms dates back many years to the time when life assurance was mainly used for the old burial policies: since you are certain to die, the proceeds were said to be assured. The question mark over the policy was not if, but when: if you lived for years, you paid for years; whereas if you died young, your burial policy could be quite a bargain. Either way, your family were *assured* of the benefits.

With other sorts of insurance, and indeed now with life assurance on premature death only, you might be lucky and not have to claim; these policies are not therefore assured, but only *insured*. Those in the business still use the separate expressions life assurance and general insurance, but few lay people bother with the distinction. However, although it is all right to talk about 'life insurance', you cannot talk about 'car assurance'. If everyone was certain to claim on his or her motor policy, the premiums would be much higher!

Where we are dealing with common fears and risks, a whole industry has developed to administer the funds, collect the premiums and pay out the claims. The insurance industry not only spreads risks between one policyholder and another; it also takes a broader view of risk. Consider the village hall again, full of a thousand young men and women paying £1 per week each. In its most simple form, if one person dies, his or her family gets £50,000, but if two died, it would only be £25,000. If they happened to have an epidemic and ten died, tough luck, it would only be £5,000 per family. That, of course, is not what people want. They want certainty that their claim will be met in full, irrespective of how many other people have a call on the fund. By paying a little more you pass the risk to the insurance company, and it loses if things turn out far worse than normal.

Common risk insurance involves thousands, or even millions, of individuals banding together. Sometimes, though, there is only one policyholder. The famous case is Betty Grable who wanted to insure her legs. Village halls full of film stars with sexy legs being hard to find, she went to Lloyd's of London who made an intelligent guess about how many people, in the normal way, lost their legs or suffered disfigurement. They were prepared to take the risk without spreading it among other policyholders.

In theory you can insure anything – the church fête being rained off, the jumbo jet crashing, the dog dying, the daily help tripping on the carpet and breaking her neck, and so on. In this chapter, we are only going to cover the main risks that private individuals face, and where there is a formalized market in policies. Special one-off deals can be struck at Lloyd's – at a price worked out by the insurance experts whose job it is to study statistics and decide what the risk is likely to be, based on past experience. With most ordinary insurance, however, you can shop around for premiums and know exactly what your position is, as along as you understand what you are doing.

Life assurance

This type may have started with the old burial policies but now there are all sorts of names attached to protection-only life insurance, quite apart from the endowment and unit-linked policies we talked about in Chapter 2 which are used for saving. (As we explained then, the ending of life assurance premium relief on policies taken out after 13 March 1984 has meant some fundamental rethinking about the whole question of linking saving to protection insurance.)

Whole life policies The most expensive policies for protection are whole life schemes, where you pay premiums usually for the whole of your life and the policy pays up when you die. Insurance companies know they will have to pay up one day, which is why the premiums are costly.

Whole life policies are not widely sold these days, except perhaps for capital transfer tax planning, when you may buy a joint life policy, which can pay out on either the first or second death. As more and more people become home-owners, with widows' rights more secure and with savings, dying in old age is not seen to present the problems it once did. Nevertheless, there are many elderly widows around for whom an insurance policy on their husbands' deaths would have made all the difference. The cost is, however, probably prohibitive for most couples if they have left it very late to take out a policy.

Term assurance A whole variety of policies are available for insuring against premature death but the fundamental principle applies – only a small proportion of policyholders will receive money out of the scheme and most will pay simply for peace of mind. The basic idea is called term assurance; you pay for a set term and, if you die within that term, your family collect the sum assured – a figure you are told at the outset. Term assurance is very, very cheap as long as the term you wish to cover does not run you into the sort of age bracket where people are likely to die from natural causes. As a guideline, a young man can buy cover of £50,000 to last until his children leave school for about £1 a week. Protection insurance, however, has been used as a loss leader to attract people into the more expensive savings policies. Without the benefit of tax relief on the premiums, savings may be directed elsewhere and the result will almost certainly be a rise in the cost of pure protection.

There are many variations on the theme of term assurance. The first is called *convertible term*. By paying a little more you get the right to extend the term or change the nature of the policy, without having to provide medical evidence. Even if you had a heart attack when you were 40, you could still convert a term policy to get cover that you might otherwise be denied. If you do exercise the right to convert to an endowment or whole life policy with much higher premiums, you will not now be given tax relief on the extra premiums.

Then there is *decreasing term*, where the purpose of the

policy is to cover perhaps the balance of an outstanding mortgage – a figure which should fall over the life of the loan. Decreasing term policies are often sold as mortgage protection policies to match in with repayment mortgages. With term assurance you may choose to have the benefits paid out as a tax-free income for the balance of the term, rather than as a lump sum. A further variation is to have it written as a family income benefit policy (known as FIB), paying out say £5,000 a year to your family until the children are grown up. This FIB policy is cheap because the older you get (and the more likely to claim) the less the proceeds will be.

In inflationary times decreasing policies are less attractive than they used to be since protection-only policies are all without profits, so benefits are eroded by inflation. Probably the best plan is that known as a *renewable convertible increasable term* – the aim being that you can increase, or extend, the cover to match inflation without evidence of health.

Non-smokers One of the main health questions from the insurance company is 'Do you smoke?' If not, insurance against premature death can be up to 25 per cent cheaper.

Insuring a wife's life One final point on cover for early death: do not think the only person whose life has a value is the husband. If he dies, all sorts of schemes may come into play – such as the company death-in-service scheme, or widows' rights under self-employed pension plans, while the state pays a regular income for widowed mothers, and indeed any widow whose husband dies once she is over 40. A wife with no dependent children who loses her husband when she is between 40 and 50 gets scaled-down widow's benefit. But widowers have no comparable benefits.

The loss of a wife can result in very considerable extra costs and, as more and more wives are also becoming joint breadwinners, there can be the loss of prospective income as well. Women have a longer average life expectancy than men; for that reason they count as 4 years younger than their male counterparts for life insurance. If protection-only is cheap for men, it is also very good value for women.

Insurance for sickness and disability
Most sensible people make provision to look after their families in the event of the death of the breadwinner. Insuring against

disablement or serious illness is less often considered, even though the financial consequences can be devastating and support from national insurance far from generous.

Nonetheless it is important to take account of what the state will pay through various benefits for sickness and for disability. Some state benefits depend on contributions, some are means-tested and some are taxable, and of course the actual level of payments is revised every November. From 1983 employers were required to pay the first 8 weeks of sickness under the statutory sick pay scheme, and many have more generous arrangements to safeguard their employees, so that a young man suddenly struck down by illness could receive as much as two thirds of his pay for the rest of his life. Details should be checked individually with your own employer. Where possible, membership of a group scheme – whether it be accident, permanent health, or for private hospital treatment – buys cover more cheaply than going it alone.

Permanent health insurance   The main drawback in the field of health insurance is the number of restrictions that are imposed. Women have to pay higher premiums than men for permanent health insurance (PHI), and certain 'disabilities' are excluded (pregnancy being one); there is also a deferred period of anything from 4 weeks to 1 year before any payment will be made. To some extent this is a matter of choice and is dictated by the level of premiums, which will also, of course, determine the size of the benefit and which should be periodically reviewed. The maximum benefits you can buy are restricted to three quarters of your earnings less state benefits, to deter claimants from malingering.

Then there is the problem of taxation. Under a group scheme the payments will be regarded as earned income and therefore subject to PAYE in the usual way; but individual PHI benefits, although they are not taxed at all for 1 full tax year (which could mean up to 23 months), are thereafter treated as unearned income, but happily that no longer involves the possibility of paying the investment income surcharge on what is effectively replacement of earnings.

Accident insurance   Unlike PHI, which pays out for the duration of any disability, accident insurance will usually have a time limit for regular payments, and they will in any case be very much more modest (usually £10 or £20 a week). The main purpose of this kind of policy is to provide a lump sum in the event of death or loss of a limb or an eye; the cost is very low, at about £1 per £1,000 of cover per year, and policies can be taken out by people up to the age of 70 without any extra loading – something to bear in mind for older people where life insurance begins to look expensive. At a time when hardly a day goes by without reading of some major road, rail or air crash, quite apart from domestic hazards, it seems a small price to pay for peace of mind.

Private health insurance   Despite the strong undercurrent of political disapproval, private health schemes have gone from strength to strength and it is now estimated that more than four million people are covered by some sort of insurance for medical treatment outside the state system. The main advantage of the schemes is that they guarantee medical treatment when and where you need it. This avoids waiting lists which can stretch for months or even years in the National Health Service. Private health schemes provide for the cost of a private hospital bed (or a private bed in a National Health hospital), consultant's and surgeon's fees and the various other expenses involved, which can easily add up to £1,000 for a routine operation and a week in hospital. In London, the figure could be much higher.

Most schemes charge according to the level of cover required and the age of the subscriber. There is an extra charge where wife and children are included but a substantial discount for members of group schemes, which in fact make up the bulk of those insured. Some employers provide free membership, although it is a taxable benefit.

Partial medical cover   As the cost of medical treatment has escalated, however, so the move from total to partial cover has developed. The luxury of instant treatment can cost £600 a year in premiums, and so some organizations have devised a compromise. If you can get the operation done on the National Health within 6 or 8 weeks, well and good; if not, the insurance takes over and you become a private patient. This development has also enabled cover to be offered to people over retirement age, always excluding existing conditions and long-stay geriatric requirements.

An alternative scheme provides cash payments for people who have to go into hospital; this should never be seen as a means of getting private medical treatment on the cheap, despite what the advertising copy might lead you to believe. Premiums are relatively small (usually less than £1 a week) and payments are anything up to £20 per day spent in hospital. Whether they are value for money is a matter of opinion, when you bear in mind that the average stay in hospital is only a week and it is reckoned that only 1 in 13 people will spend time as an in-patient each year.

House insurance
For most people, their home will represent the most valuable asset they own, and it makes no sense to skimp on the cost of insuring it. If it is damaged by fire or by flood, if the pipes burst or the central heating explodes, with decent protection you will not be landed personally with a bill for thousands of pounds.

Anyone who has a mortgage will, of course, be required by the building society or whoever lends the money to provide proper buildings insurance. It is as well to remember that the lender is interested only in making sure the loan is secure in the event of a disaster. He is not concerned whether you also have the correct cover to replace a set of silver cutlery or repair a cigarette burn in the Persian rug: both items covered by your contents, as opposed to your buildings, policy.

Much of the confusion about house insurance results from not knowing precisely what is covered by the policy and the extent to which it is covered. Three of the most important misunderstandings are the amount of the *excess*, which usually requires the policyholder to meet the first £20 or £50 of any claim; *averaging*, which means if you under-insure the property, the company may well decide to pay out only a percentage of the claim; and *wear and tear*, which means that there may well be a reduction because new materials are used to replace something which had already seen a part of its useful life.

Some insurance companies have gone to considerable lengths to write their policies in simple English, setting out the technical cover on one side in precise legal jargon and then explaining on the opposite page what it means in practice. This has helped to remove the suspicion that companies are out to word their policies in such a way that they will not have to pay out when the time comes, but there is no substitute for reading small print and, if in doubt, asking precisely what is excluded. Not every policy, for example, covers flooding or subsidence (which caused havoc in the mid-1970s) and in certain areas you may be required to pay extra (what is called *loading*), if the insurance company thinks there is a greater risk; living near a river would be an obvious example. There is also the possibility that the excess will be greater for certain problems such as subsidence, which may be expressed as a percentage of the claim rather than as a flat amount.

Valuing for insurance   If you ask a man what his home is worth, he will probably mention a figure at which similar houses in the district have been sold. This is another common source of confusion. Because in practice a building is rarely destroyed completely, particularly by fire, most insurance claims are for partial damage, so the insurance company will assess value in terms of rebuilding costs, not the open-market value of the property. Provided that the house is relatively new and constructed of modern materials, the difference between what you can sell it for and what it would cost to rebuild may not be significant; with older properties, or those with special architectural features, there may be a huge discrepancy.

Calculating rebuilding costs   It is relatively simple to calculate rebuilding costs with the help of free leaflets supplied either by the insurance company or by the British Insurance Association. These are regularly updated in line with what builders actually charge in various parts of the country for typical detached, semi-detached or terrace properties in different age groups. Calculate the floor space, multiply by the cost per square foot (which may be anything between £25 and £50), add on something for demolition, architect's fees and sundries and any fixtures and fittings, and you should have the correct sum.

The problems start when this figure is twice what you know the property is actually worth; it is hard to explain why £60,000 of cover is insufficient on a Victorian terrace house which was bought for that amount but which would cost three times as much to rebuild, especially as you cannot simply walk away from your liability to make good the damage.

There is also a popular misconception that, if the house burnt down, the insurance money could be used to buy another one. This may not in fact be legally practicable or possible. This is one of the reasons why most companies are unwilling to offer cover on what is called the *first loss principle*, which means that you can claim up to a certain amount regardless of what the damage is or how it was caused and (at least in theory) carry the rest of the risk yourself. The other reason is that premiums are calculated on the average size of the claims, and if everyone was under-insured by a half, premiums would have to double.

Building insurance covers what are commonly referred to as the principal perils: fire, lightning, explosions, riots and so on, which may cause damage to fabric, but there are some grey areas – notably where gates, fences and garden sheds are concerned. It is your duty to keep the house in reasonable repair and, in the event of any claim, to do what you can to minimize the damage and undertake any temporary work that may be necessary. Depending on the size of the claim, the insurance company may or may not send along a loss adjuster to decide what it will or will not pay out, but in any event you will have to get proper estimates, and you cannot expect the insurance to cover what may well be seen as improvements.

Despite what you may have heard to the contrary, an adjuster is a neutral observer; although his fees are paid by the insurance company, he has to maintain strict professional standards of impartiality. Indeed, since his purpose is to achieve a just and fair settlement, he is quite likely to point out items which you have costed or valued too low, as well as any work which may not fall within the scope of your cover. If the claim is large or complex, the owner can always hire his own loss assessor as a representative. A good assessor will almost certainly be able to justify his fees by taking care of all the points of detail, doing the paperwork as well as talking the same language as the adjuster.

The cost of building insurance The cost of insuring the building, as opposed to the contents of your home, has changed relatively little over the years in percentage terms and, depending on the precise extent of the cover, will be somewhere between £1.25 and £1.80 per £1,000. The cash outlay will, of course, escalate as the value and the rebuilding costs rise. Some companies will automatically adjust the sum insured each year, but, even if they do, check the calculations for yourself every so often in the light of local conditions. There is also usually a nominal premium to be paid for £250,000 or £500,000 of personal liability cover, in case someone is injured on your premises, but make sure you check this too.

Building society cover As a condition of the loan, building societies will insist on the buildings being covered. They used to specify which company you had to use, and in the process made sure of collecting commission on the deal. Nowadays, the borrower is generally allowed to use any company he likes, although there may be a small extra charge by the society for administration.

Building societies are now increasingly offering package deals which include not only the cover for the buildings but also cover for a specified amount of contents; they are in effect buying bulk cover. You may find the contents part of the deal much cheaper than doing it separately, especially if you live in a high-risk urban area. To cut down on administration most societies opt for what is regarded as the typical furniture and possessions of an average family. This could be set at half the value of the building or it could be calculated on a room by room basis. In any event, since contents insurance can now cost as much as £11 or £12 per £1,000 of sum insured in the big cities, it is well worth exploring any possibility of savings, provided the cover is adequate.

Insuring the contents of your home

Most contents insurance is now done on what is called a *new for old* basis, meaning that if an article is stolen or destroyed you will be paid the replacement value to buy something brand new. There are exceptions to this, in the case of clothing and household linen, but in the main this type of cover means that you need not worry about rising prices, as long as the contents are correctly valued in the first place. The alternative is to buy *indemnity* insurance, where you will be paid replacement cost minus an allowance for wear and tear. In this case, if your hi-fi has a useful life of 10 years, and it is stolen after 5 years, you would only get half the money needed to replace it, whereas 'new for old' would pick up the whole bill. Some companies offer hybrid policies, which are a mixture of new for old and indemnity but it is important to be quite clear what items fall into which category.

Limitations of contents policies   It is also important to understand the limitations of contents policies. Most contents policies do not cover accidental damage, such as a valuable vase being knocked off the mantelpiece by the cat, or a lump of red hot coal burning a hole in the carpet; and they certainly do not cover the loss of a ring or a camera once you take it out of the house. Indeed, even inside the house the cover on 'valuables' may be limited to a specified percentage of the total sum insured. What you need in this case is an *all risks* insurance so that the items are covered regardless of what happens or where you are at the time, and even this may be restricted to anywhere within the United Kingdom, not outside it. While 'all risks' is usually thought of in terms of jewellery, it is also useful for replacing such things as clothing damaged by an accident or, more commonly, a suitcase of clothes and personal belongings which may be stolen from your car. An alternative claim on the car insurance could jeopardize your 'no claims' bonus.

'No claims' bonuses almost never extend to housing and despite the great increase in burglary there is little financial encouragement to invest in expensive forms of protection. Indeed most companies will make it a condition to giving above-average cover on valuables that you install special door and window locks and quite possibly an alarm system as well. Any discounts on premiums are likely to be modest and the company concerned may not be the most competitive in the market, even with a discount.

Valuing special items   The most important precautions are, firstly, to be able to identify an item if it is stolen and, secondly, to have a reasonable idea of its value. It is sensible to make a list of your valuables with a proper description which will be useful in the event of a claim, as well as helping police to recover the goods if stolen. Nowadays the big auction houses will usually give a free valuation even if you have no intention of selling, provided that you take the article to them, although they will charge a fee if you want the value set out formally for insurance purposes. Remember also that there may be a substantial difference between what a gold watch, for instance, is worth if you sell it secondhand, and what its insurance value will be if you have to replace it new. Personal experience has shown the two figures could be as much as £800 on the one hand and as little as £250 on the other.

Disputing a claim   What do you do if your claim is either turned down or only partially met by the company, so that you find yourself in dispute? Correspondence in the media shows the strength of feeling that this can arouse, but people often forget the first and most necessary course of action – to find out precisely on what grounds the company has acted. It may be that the risk simply was not covered. It may be a misunderstanding of the precise legal wording of the policy. In any event insurance companies, or most of them, no longer act as judge and jury and there is recourse either to the Insurance Ombudsman or to an alternative system, known as the Personal Insurance Arbitration Service (PIAS), which is run through the Chartered Institute of Arbitrators (see Appendix for address).

Although the Ombudsman only started operations in 1981, and his office is funded by the companies themselves, he has built up an impressive record in sorting out some of the more intractable disputes and while his judgements are binding on the companies, the individual may still resort to the law if he wishes. It should be pointed out, incidentally, that most aspects of life insurance are not covered by the Ombudsman.

Car insurance

Compared to house insurance, the car insurance market is an absolute jungle. Several years of intense competition have produced such a variety of discounts, concessions and special deals from companies, that only a broker with access to the computerized QUOTEL system is likely to make any sense of your own individual circumstances. That is not to say that you can simply hand the whole problem over and ignore the fundamentals. Motor insurance is a legal requirement and a driver must have minimum statutory cover against liability to third parties, including passengers in the vehicle he or she is driving. In fact, very few motorists will choose this minimum cover unless convictions for motoring offences give them no choice or they are very young.

Limited cover   The commonest cover for those on a limited budget, which usually means they are driving an older car, is third party, fire and theft. The *third party* in this case also takes care of damage to other vehicles or property, but not the damage to your own car. If you are involved in an accident which is not your fault, you have to claim against the other driver's insurance, which is sometimes easier said than done. The first and second parties, incidentally, are the policyholder and the insurance company.

Comprehensive cover   Damage to your own car is covered by a comprehensive policy and this can be extended to other named drivers or people driving with your permission. This type of cover pays up to a limited extent in the event of articles which may be stolen from the car while it is parked (though beware the loss of 'no claims' bonus). It also enables the policyholder to drive other vehicles which he does not own (though usually only with third party cover), and one of the leading companies in the field also offers free car hire for a limited period in the event of your own being off the road after an accident.

Premium costs Obviously a comprehensive policy costs considerably more than third party cover, but there are so many variables that one driver can end up paying £20 or £30 while another has to fork out £200 or £300. In fact insurance companies divide cars into a number of rating groups from 1−7 with a small British family hatchback rated at the bottom of the scale and a continental limousine or sports car at the top. The scale rates may also vary between particular models, insurers being very wary of 'souped up' versions and left-hand drive models, and, since the cost of repairing an imported car is almost invariably higher than for one produced in Britain, this will also be reflected. As well as the make and model of car, the insurance company will need to know in which area it is kept − with the highest risk in central London and the lowest in remote rural localities. The age and the occupation of the driver will be taken into consideration, the number of years of driving experience, and of course any previous accidents or convictions.

All these factors will determine the basic premium to be charged, but that is not the end of the story. The driver who can show an accident-free record will have built up a *no claim bonus* which can over 4 years reduce the cost by up to 60 per cent. He can choose to protect that no claim bonus so that it (or part of it) is not lost in the event of one or two claims. There is a discount for owner-only cover, or husband and wife. Anyone prepared voluntarily to pay a larger than normal part of any claim (£50 or £100 for example), instead of the usual excess of £25, will get a discount. In addition, in an attempt to identify (and profit from) lower-risk business, several insurers will offer concessionary terms to older drivers (usually those over 50) or those whose annual mileage is below certain limits, perhaps 5,000 or 10,000 miles. Owners of vintage or classic cars can also benefit substantially from low mileage cover through special policies which will not dispute the rarity value. On the other hand, if your car is not garaged, or if you want to teach your 17-year-old son or daughter to drive, then you must expect to pay more. Small wonder that the only way to make sense of it is to use a broker and make it quite clear precisely which limitations you are prepared to put up with.

Warranty insurance   One thing that is not covered by comprehensive car insurance is the cost of a major breakdown. In this case what is needed is extended warranty insurance of the kind provided by the motoring organizations. The schemes supplement the manufacturer's guarantee, but they are not cheap and there are restrictions on the age of the car and the total mileage, as well as a requirement to pay the first part of any claim and possibly a limit on the total claim or number of claims you can make.

Other long-term insurance cover

Once life and health, home and car, have been dealt with, for most people there is little else to worry about. In any case there is a limit to the amount of money that can be paid out in premiums. There is a risk in almost every human activity and it has to be a matter of temperament (and means) as to whether you take it, or pass it on to an underwriter.

Legal insurance   One area which is growing increasingly popular is cover for legal expenses. The immense cost of going to court and the limitations of legal aid mean that unless you are very wealthy you may not be able to pursue your rights through the courts. This type of cover has always been commonplace in Europe but has been slow to catch on in Britain. Arguments with shopkeepers, garages or builders over bills and service are perhaps the commonest source of discontent, but there are various proceedings which are excluded from insurance cover, including criminal proceedings, divorces and disputes with the Inland Revenue, and naturally, you cannot obtain help with pre-existing cases.

Although some companies provide cover in an all-embracing policy (and there is one which can be added to normal household insurance), others have sub-divided cover between household and motor with separate specialist cover available to landlords, shopkeepers and so on. One of the most useful features of these policies is a 24-hour hotline to someone who will be able to explain what courses of action are open to you and whether or not you have a case.

Short-term insurance

So far we have been talking about continuous cover for long periods of time, but there are occasions when people will want short-term insurance, for example when moving house, hiring a car, or going on holiday. Most people will probably use the cover suggested by the removal firm, the car hire company or the tour operator, but it is sensible, firstly, to check that there are no undue restrictions and, secondly, that better cover cannot be obtained in the open market. Policy conditions can vary widely, especially in the travel business, and it is important to make sure that they are realistic for the place you are going to, the time you are planning to spend away, and the value of the possessions you are taking with you.

Holiday insurance   Following a good deal of adverse publicity in the late 1970s, holiday insurance has been greatly improved. In particular the medical limits have been increased to £100,000 or more to take care of North America, and claims should now be met for all the obvious risks, like loss or theft of luggage and money, accidents or cancellation through no fault of your own, delays and personal liability.

Car insurance abroad depends on where you are going, and you should let your insurer know as soon as possible about your plans, especially if you are planning to go outside Europe. In order to ensure that you have the same level of cover as you have at home, you must obtain a Green Card, which is an internationally recognized insurance document giving evidence of the fact that your British insurance policy provides the necessary cover within EEC countries, some of which require more than Britain and some of which have less stringent requirements. The motoring organizations will also be able to assist with practical information on driving abroad, including procedures after an accident.

The range of other insurance policies is almost endless, but some that might be considered useful to the average householder include cover for pets, jury service, multiple births, weather and a whole list of sporting activities. There are also specialist policies for elderly people seeking low-cost house insurance, flat-dwellers, and students wishing to insure their belongings at college. But being over-insured is just as silly as being under-insured. Consider the risks you run and how often; then check you are not duplicating existing cover.

131

Chapter 9

THE FAMILY FINANCIAL UNIT

We've nothing against women - we just don't lend them money...

Benefits and penalties for women

In most areas of finance there is little difference between the advice given to women and to men; there are, however, some special factors for women to watch out for. We have already pointed out that women live longer than men. The advantage from a financial point of view is that life assurance is cheaper to buy, but the problems come when you combine a woman's greater longevity with the fact that on average she will be about 3 years younger than her husband. That could mean widowhood for between 5 and 10 years; in the past this has resulted in many elderly women being among our poorest citizens, trying to cope with all the increasingly difficult problems of old age and loneliness, with very little money.

This problem may never be cured completely but at least widows' pensions are now compulsory in company pension schemes. The increasing move to home ownership should also mean that elderly widows will have a roof over their heads, and are less likely to be at the mercy of neglectful private landlords. With joint homes, joint mortgages and often joint earnings, women are learning to be more self reliant, and none too soon: even without a divorce it is almost certain that there will be no man to help when many big decisions have to be taken.

The mention of widows' pensions brings to mind one subject where many working wives feel they are treated as second-class breadwinners. Why is there not a standard range of death benefits for widowers? Part of the reason is that pensions are run on old-fashioned lines; wives are protected because they are thought of as dependants. Husbands are not assumed to be dependent on their wives and, indeed, it is not conventionally thought manly for them to be. But the truth is that these days couples are increasingly financially interdependent on each other. Until such time as the pensions industry modernizes its thinking, it is better to take out extra life cover for the wife than simply complain at the unfairness of it all.

Disadvantages of PHI cover One policy which does seem to be unfair on women is permanent health insurance, where women are asked to pay higher premiums than men. If women are considered to be so frail (vulnerable to long-term illness), how is it that they live so long? It may be that statistics are inadequate for wives. It may be that insurance companies reckon that given half a chance women would all malinger and go back to the kitchen, where at heart they think women yearn to be. But they are now being tested in the courts by women's groups and will have to find some strong actuarial arguments to keep up the discrimination. Even so, it may take several years to resolve this problem.

Pensions In terms of pensions, women have a problem. In order to entice them back to work in World War II, they were given a retirement age of 60, 5 years younger than men. In fact, it has not worked out too badly since in many households, a wife reaches 60 only a year or so before her husband retires at

65. If you equalize the retirement age without changing marriage habits, you are going to get some working wives, in their late fifties, who are determinedly hanging on to their jobs while their husbands are cooking and shopping and drawing pensions. However, a retirement age of 60 does mean that on a sixtieths scheme, a woman has little chance of getting to the two thirds maximum pension that a man might. Taking time off to have children does not help, although the new state scheme gives credit for home responsibility.

Until 1977, working wives were allowed to opt out of many state benefits; by going for a reduced rate of contributions, they could give up the right to unemployment benefit and a pension in their own right. That option has now been scrapped except for wives who chose that route before April 1977 and maintained it with no more than a 2-year break in work ever since.

Even if you are one of the small band of women with the option, it may still pay to give it up now, particularly if making full contributions would bring your total number of contributory years up to more than a quarter of your working life, so giving you some pension at age 60. The *overlapping benefit rules* do not allow a married couple to get two pensions: overlapping benefits are those in which two different situations would justify benefit such as sickness and unemployment. You get the greater of the two. Thus a wife with her own pension cannot also qualify as a dependant of her husband and he would only be able to draw an allowance to the extent that his wife's pension fell short of the dependant's allowance. You have to work out which is best, and you have only one chance a year to change your mind, just before the beginning of the tax year. See Chapter 7.

Income tax　The retirement age has effectively been equalized for tax purposes – but at 65. That is when the age allowance comes into play and this bears very heavily on the single woman, or widow, whose state pension wipes out all her tax-free allowance until she reaches 65.

In the year of marriage, on the other hand, a wife wins hands down. For the husband the extra personal allowance is scaled down on a pro-rata basis: in other words he loses one twelfth of the extra allowance for each month he is unmarried during the tax year. The bride, however, is literally cut into two taxpayers in the year of marriage, each receiving full allowances, assuming she goes on working. Neither is her investment income added to her husband's in that year. Thereafter, interest and dividends on her savings will be taxed as if they were her husband's.

It may seem unfair but, if it were not done this way, the husband could use his wife as a tax haven now that transferring assets between spouses produces no capital transfer or gains tax problems. A wife's earnings can be taxed separately, but it does not pay to split up for tax purposes until together you would each be into the higher-rate tax bracket. This is fully explained in Chapter 5.

Savings If a wife wishes to keep her savings secret from her husband she should use national savings certificates, which are free of all tax; more importantly, they do not have to be declared to the Inland Revenue. A building society share account might seem a better source of interest, but even though there is no extra tax for basic-rate payers, the Revenue should be notified in case it affects higher-rate tax liability, and this would destroy the element of secrecy.

Discrimination Over the past few years many institutions have fallen over backwards not to discriminate against women. Building societies, for example, try very hard to be fair on mortgages, talking of the main breadwinner with a mortgage of up to 2½ times earnings and the secondary earner at 1 times income and turning a blind eye to the fact that young wives may well stop work to have children. But not all women choose to marry these days. For single women, the main improvement has been an increasing equality of opportunity in the more interesting and well-paid jobs. The move to equal pay may leave something to be desired but at least the idea is dying out that if a woman's place cannot be in the home, it ought to be in the typing pool.

Single women, and particularly the better paid, are a fruitful potential market for life insurance and financial services designed specifically with women in mind. Endless refinements are added to basic products to make good marketing copy but in truth it all costs virtually nothing to put together and is often only window dressing. If you want a savings plan or protection policy, you should really take equality to its logical conclusion and ignore the fact you are female at all.

Living together   Not being married does not, of course, necessitate living alone. More and more couples are living together without the legal bond of marriage these days, mostly because they see little point in wedlock at that stage in their lives. Some do it, though, to gain financial advantage, such as the fact that the woman's investment income is not aggregated with her man's, that they can each get up to £30,000 of mortgage interest tax relief, and that they can even covenant money to their 'step-children' under age 18, and be treated as 'single parents' with separate tax allowances.

But there are snags. The CTT exemptions on transfers between spouses do not apply to common law wives. They will not be protected by intestacy rules if one partner dies without making a will, and, if the relationship breaks up, there are no clear guidelines about who should have what. Postponing marriage may be sensible for many reasons, but if it goes on for too long, it could lead to financial problems.

Saving for children and for students

One of Britain's big insurance companies has calculated that the cost of bringing up a child can be well over £100,000 and that makes no allowance for inflation. Admittedly, nearly half of this is represented by the potential loss of the woman's earnings and about a third for private education. But the survey showed how the costs escalated from about 8 per cent of income in the first year of the child's life to more than 25 per cent between the ages of 15 and 17. Half the parents interviewed said they experienced some financial problems, but 4 out of 5 said that the expense had not caused them to postpone starting a family.

In fact, with sensible planning, it is possible to reduce costs quite substantially and at the same time give the child some insight into how to look after money. Even before the child is born the woman should have checked up on her rights to maternity benefit and, of course, her rights to continuing employment if that is what she wants. From the time the child is born until it reaches the age of 19 or ceases to be in full-time education there will be the weekly receipt of child benefit, which is entirely tax-free.

Covenants for children under 18   Probably the first question to be asked once the baby is born is whether there are grandparents, aunts or uncles who may be prepared to enter into a covenant. One of the concessions in the tax system is that everyone is entitled to his or her own personal allowance regardless of age, which means a useful chunk of tax-free income. Assuming that the donor has sufficient taxable income, the tax paid can then be reclaimed by the parents on the child's behalf, turning each annual payment of £100 into £142.80. This means that more than £600 will be returned by the taxman for the child's benefit according to the personal allowance for 1984–85 of £2,005.

Unfortunately it is not possible for the parents themselves to make deeds of covenant to their own children until they reach the age of 18 (although arrangements can be made by unmarried couples) and the covenant must be able to run for at least 7 years (as opposed to charitable covenants, which can be limited to 4 years). This is not to say that the covenant has to run for 7 years; it may in fact go on for a shorter or longer period, but it is legally enforceable.

Very often covenants are used to build up money for school fees and in this case there used to be a further bonus in that an additional 15 per cent of life assurance premium relief was added once the child had reached the age of 12. In this way an original payment of £1,000 is increased to £1,428 by reclaiming the 30 per cent basic-rate tax (there is, incidentally, no covenant relief against higher-rate tax); it then got a further boost to £1,680 by life assurance premium relief. Although the Budget stopped premium relief for new policies, when a child under the age of 12 has a policy, he or she will get the tax relief from the age of 12.

School fees Much specialist advice is now available on school fees planning, whether it is through covenants or by contributions direct from the parents. Some depend on straightforward life assurance, others on more complicated systems involving charitable trusts, but the message in every case is to start as young as you can.

For parents hoping to spread the burden of fees by using life assurance, the loss of tax relief on new policies will make this more difficult. It probably only makes sense now for higher-rate taxpayers and even then only if the policy can run for at least 10 years before the fees are due to be paid. If you have left it very late, beware of schemes involving loans. There is no tax relief against the loan interest, the interest rate itself is often high, and repayment is usually made via an insurance policy, where there is now, of course, no tax relief. If a lump sum is available, for example from grandparents, then there is a great deal more flexibility in using the capital transfer tax exempt band and then drawing up a tailormade investment plan in the child's name, but you will need professional advice for this.

National savings   But what about the child's own savings? Invariably there will be birthday and Christmas presents, there may also be larger sums perhaps in the form of legacies. Provided these do not derive from the parents there is no problem with any income that accrues within the level of the personal tax allowance, and investment can be undertaken balancing convenience against the best possible return. In the case of parental gifts, the rule (long overdue for reform) is that any interest over £5 has to be added to parents' income for tax purposes, so the usual choice in this case is national savings certificates, which are free of all tax.

Most people will think initially of the National Savings Bank for relatively small sums of money. The ordinary account is useful for small amounts, and since the child is able to operate the account alone from the age of 7, it gives an early sense of responsibility. Unfortunately the interest rate of 3 per cent is hardly spectacular (even with the first £70 of interest tax-free). However, if there is at least £500 in the account for a full calendar year, 6 per cent is paid.

The investment account is probably the most tax efficient and easily operated alternative. It can be opened on the child's behalf and the child can take over at age 7. It invariably pays a highly competitive rate of interest without deduction of tax, and now that the interest is accumulated on a daily basis there is no more nonsense about having to keep money in for whole calendar months. Lastly, the fact that a month's notice has to be given for withdrawals is unlikely to prove a problem.

Building societies and banks   It is usually suggested that children should choose banks rather than building societies for their savings because the tax deducted by building societies cannot be reclaimed. While this is still true until April 1985, there may not be a great deal of difference between the two rates of interest. Indeed since the middle of 1983, net building society rates have been consistently above gross rates paid by the big high street clearing banks. But if we are talking about having fun and developing the savings habit, then it really matters very little which you choose, and it is rather hard on a child who badly wants a Snoopy, or a Paddington Bear, or a Mickey Mouse money box to use tax as the excuse for not complying. Once children have reached their teens, there is also something to be said for starting to build up a track record with a building society in anticipation that one day they may need a mortgage.

Unit trusts and life assurance   Where larger sums of money are involved or there is a regular commitment to put aside £10 or £20 a month over a long period, then one should look at some form of risk investment. The simplest idea nowadays is almost certainly a unit trust savings scheme, though you should remember that the child will not be able to get at the proceeds until the age of 14.

An alternative used to be to take out a child's endowment policy, but the child could not obtain a premium relief until the age of 12. As this has now been scrapped, and in any case the life cover was largely irrelevant, the idea has been overtaken by events. Existing policies, where the child is over the age of 12, are not affected, though the child cannot cash the policy in until the age of 17 or 18.

Covenants for the over-18s   As soon as the child reaches the age of 18, the parents are completely free to enter into a covenant, and, indeed, the Inland Revenue now make this much easier by supplying a ready-made form, IR47. This is especially useful in helping to put a child through university. But watch out for traps. For example, the student's own part-time earnings could be taxable if you used the full allowance on a covenant. If the student does not pay tax, you are pushing your child into the black economy at an early age.

Student grants   Parental covenants (but not those from other relatives) are ignored completely in working out the entitlement to a grant, which is based on income. Over about £7,000 and up to perhaps £25,000, the grant entitlement works on a sliding scale. Each academic year's grant will be fixed by reference to the parents' income in the preceding tax year, so plan ahead and get the relevant leaflet from your local authority or from the Department of Education and Science. That way you can at least budget, if not manoeuvre a little more grant by careful financial planning. Putting a son or daughter through university is an expensive business even though tuition nowadays is free, and the minimum grant for undergraduates is now only £205.

Child's trust   Finally there is one little-known loophole which does make it possible for a parent to settle money on the child through a trust in which the money belongs to the child absolutely, and for tax to be avoided on the income (up to the personal allowance limit of £2,005), provided that the income is allowed to accumulate until the child is 18. If, however, anything whatsoever is spent for the child's benefit including any tax rebates, then that money must be added to the parents' income for the purposes of tax assessment. You will need professional advice to ensure that the trust deed is correctly drawn up.

Finance for the elderly

The biggest worry facing many elderly people is that they will somehow run out of money, or their income will decline to a point where they can no longer make ends meet. When inflation runs in double figures it is a justifiable fear, and yet the immediate solution — to seek the highest possible return on their savings — may be self-defeating.

Obviously there are no hard and fast rules. Some people may find themselves with a lump sum and a pension of several thousand pounds a year from their job, on top of the state pension, which is of course uprated in line with inflation every year. They may have substantial capital and, rather than investing it for their own benefit, their problem may be how to pass it on with the minimum liability to capital transfer tax. Others may find themselves relying heavily on the state through means-tested supplementary benefit, housing benefit and payments for invalidity or mobility. It may be that the elderly person has a valuable house, but very little in the way of cash to invest, or the problem may be to find some sort of sheltered or supervised accommodation, either in the private sector or run by a local authority.

A man aged 65 has a further life expectancy of around 14 years and women may live until well over the age of 80. If you remember the formula for calculating the effects of inflation

(70 divided by the rate of inflation = the number of years in which the value of money halves), you will be able to get your affairs in better perspective. The elderly do have certain advantages: for example, they usually enjoy cheap transport and concessions on a variety of services, such as hairdressing and cinemas, at off-peak times. They are given an increased personal tax allowance at age 65 which results in a higher tax-free income; for 1984–85 this is £2,490 for a single pensioner and £3,955 for a couple, subject to the income limit of £8,100, which is fully explained in Chapter 5.

Working after retirement age   Some people aim to go on working at least part-time beyond the normal retirement age. As long as your income does not breach the *earnings rule* you will not suffer any penalties. If, however, your income (after certain expenses) exceeds £65 a week, then you start to lose part of your state pension at the rate of 5p for every 10p earned; above £69 and it disappears at 5p for every 5p. From this you can calculate that a single person's pension can be wiped out completely if you earn just over £100 a week and there is no point in drawing it at all. Better to defer it and collect additional pension when you finally do decide to retire. This accrues at the rate of 1p in the pound for each 7 weeks that you do not draw your pension and works out at just over 7½ per cent a year. Married women who continue working beyond the age of 60 can lose that part of the pension paid for them on their husband's contributions, and, if you are under 60, then the earnings limit is £45. The earnings rule only applies for 5 years (i.e. 70 for men and 65 for women).

Income from savings   The most important consideration is not to be lured into some complicated scheme unless you fully understand the consequences. Our old friends, the National Savings investment account, income bond and index-linked certificates, and building society monthly income extra interest accounts may sound boring, but they should form the basis of any retired person's assets. Only when you have set aside enough for your regular commitments and for emergencies can you afford to think about risk.

If your total capital is less than about £10,000, then it is probably unwise to take any risk at all. However, if you do go for maximum income, remember that unless you set aside some of it each year to rebuild your capital, it will be eroded by inflation.

Many people do not realize that the present nominally high interest rates could not be sustained if there was no inflation. The 'true' long-term rate of interest is only about 3 per cent; the rest compensates you for the fall in capital value and, if you spend it, you are in effect dipping into that capital.

Risk investment   Probably the safest risk investment is to go for some type of managed fund, whether it be a unit or investment trust, or in certain cases an investment bond. Guaranteed income bonds should be treated with caution, following the end of life assurance premium relief. The longer-term ones used to rely quite heavily on tax relief to restore the capital at the end of the term, and the fact that this is no longer available means less can be set aside to provide the income.

Banks, stockbrokers and insurance brokers will be able to assess the market for you but remember they have to live by commission and so their advice does not come free. In the last couple of years stock markets round the world have had a marvellous run, so the performance of bonds and trusts has been impressive, but the past is no guide to the future. In any event you will certainly start with a much lower income even if you choose income-orientated funds, unless they are con-fined to government securities or other fixed interest schemes.

A scheme which has attracted wide attention is the one in which 'income' is stripped out of government securities or local authority yearling bonds by selling them just before the interest payment is due. The resultant capital gain is only subject to tax at 30 per cent and, bearing in mind the current capital gains tax-free allowance of £5,600, this means that many people will not be affected. Although the scheme has been tested in court and the Inland Revenue lost its case for taxing the gain as if it was income, this could always be changed by future legislation. The Revenue can also assess the gain to higher-rate tax, though in practice this rarely seems to happen, and there is an outside chance of being treated as a trader. The schemes are well known to brokers and profes-sional advisers, and are for all practical purposes very low risk, but you should still make sure you understand what you are doing.

A home income plan   One idea that tempts many elderly people who find themselves with a valuable house, but short of income, is to take out a home income plan. What happens is that you mortgage your house and use the proceeds to buy an annuity. Since the mortgage gets tax relief and the annuity attracts favourable tax treatment, the net result is a boost to income. Further details of how these schemes work can be found in Chapter 6.

Housing insurance On the subject of housing, you may well be able to obtain cheaper contents insurance for your furniture and valuables. The scheme is run by Age Concern, who also monitor other deals for the elderly by which expenses can be legitimately and safely reduced.

Putting your affairs in someone else's hands There comes a time when elderly people will find things are getting too much for them, and some of the responsibilities will have to be taken on by relatives. It is possible to arrange things so that the minimum confusion is caused. For example the state pension can be credited to a bank account each month, as can the income from National Savings income bonds and from building societies. It is quite straightforward to arrange for things like rates and electricity to be paid by means of standing orders or direct debits, and, provided the elderly person understands what is happening, a mandate can be given for a relative to operate a bank or building society account.

Eventually, it may become necessary for a relative to take out full power of attorney, which gives legal authority to deal with virtually any part of the elderly person's affairs, subject to supervision by the Court of Protection. The law here is not wholly satisfactory in that a power of attorney is automatically revoked when the person giving it becomes mentally incapable – just at the time when it may be most needed. Proposals have been made to change the law, subject to proper safeguards, but it remains to be seen when action will be taken.

Dealing with a death in the family

It is quite likely that many people reading this book have not made a will. Maybe you think you have too little money to bother with a will or that it does not matter if the only people involved are to be your husband, wife or children.

Intestacy In fact, dying intestate is at best a nuisance for those who have to sort out your affairs and at worst can result in your assets being distributed in a way that might be totally against your wishes (if, for example, you had separated but had not yet divorced). From the beginning of 1983, where there is no will divorce totally disinherits a former spouse. The laws of intestacy are designed to provide for your surviving spouse and for your children, with other relatives following in a certain pecking order.

If, for example, a man dies leaving an estate worth £100,000, then the wife gets the first £40,000 plus a life interest in half the rest, from which she will receive the income. The children get the balance, both capital and income, plus the capital held on trust for the widow until she dies. If she failed to make a will, then her estate would be equally divided among the children. In the case of a single person, the estate would pass first to his or her parents, then to siblings and/or their children and, failing that, by stages right down the line to the children of half-uncles or aunts.

Preparing a will It is possible to prepare your own will, provided your estate is simple, with the help of a suitable book. Printed forms are available from stationers, and as long as the will is signed, dated and witnessed correctly by two people who are not beneficiaries under the will (or married to a beneficiary), it should be effective. Since the only way to test it is by dying, the wisest course of action for most people is to consult a solicitor – it can cost as little as £25 or £30. Having made a will, it is important to keep it up to date, to remember that marriage revokes a previous will, and to make sure that there is a note of where it is kept (if in doubt, use the bank).

Executing a will It is much easier to act as an executor if there is a clearly worded will and there is, incidentally, no bar to a beneficiary being appointed as an executor; a beneficiary will have an incentive to get things sorted out quickly. The question of whether to call in professional help at this stage is generally determined by the complexity of the estate and your own willingness to tackle a personal application for probate.

Solicitors and banks have scales of fees which are related to the size of the assets and in some cases these are out of all proportion to the work involved. In the case of trusts or businesses, professional skills are indispensable. Even with a simple estate, doing it yourself may be time-consuming and slow though officialdom is generally on your side. Helpful publications are listed under Further Reading in the Appendix.

Since all assets are frozen from the date of death, it is sensible to have made some provision for ready cash, for example by having a joint bank account or an insurance policy written for the benefit of your spouse or children, who can then collect the proceeds with the minimum formalities. It is also a good idea to have the house in joint names, unless there is some positive reason for not so doing.

Probate The Probate Personal Application Department which operates within the Family Division of the High Court will supply the necessary documents; in addition to the main London office, there are various probate registries around the country which can handle personal applications. Gathering together the assets, listing them and valuing them has to be done according to certain rules, and you will also have to satisfy the Inland Revenue on any income tax liability.

If the estate is below £40,000, it will be 'excepted' from the need for a capital transfer tax account (prior to April 1983 the limit was £25,000). This does not, however, mean that you can give away large sums of money just before you die to get below the limit. Any lifetime transfers within the previous 10 years, apart from those falling within the annual exemption, will count towards the total transferred. If they were made less than 3 years before death, the higher rate of CTT, which is now twice the lifetime rate, will apply.

If the estate is less than £5,000 (the limit was raised from the £1,500 at which it had stood since 1975 and will apply to all deaths on or after 11 May 1984), then it may be possible to dispense with probate altogether, provided that the money is in such things as building societies and national savings. These organizations are not obliged to hand over small deposits; most in practice will do so on evidence of death, particularly where there is a need to pay funeral costs. The contribution from the state is a meagre £30 by way of death grant; the cost of even a modest funeral today is extremely unlikely to be less than £400.

Capital transfer tax Grant of probate (letters of administration in the case of an intestacy) cannot be given until the bill for any CTT has been settled. Surviving spouses may inherit property tax-free, thereafter the first £64,000 of an estate escapes CTT, always assuming that the deceased has not used up any of this allowance during his or her lifetime, and remembering that lifetime gifts now drop out of the reckoning after 10 years. The details of this and other exemptions can be found in Chapter 5, while the current thresholds and rates will be found in the Tables in the Appendix. If CTT is payable on property which remains unsold, you are allowed to pay by annual instalments though interest will be charged on the outstanding balance.

Making your will tax-efficient Although it is sensible for any-one with an estate well in excess of £64,000 to make sure it is distributed in a tax-efficient way after death (and there is plenty of professional advice around for the asking), it is possible to change the terms of a will under what is called a *deed of family arrangement*. This enables the beneficiaries to rearrange the bequests in such a way as to minimize tax or take care of some particular members of the family, as long as anyone receiving less than the will states is happy to agree and there are no children under the age of 18 involved. This can also be done to override the rules of intestacy, provided all the parties are in agreement. Give some consideration to leaving money to charity, particularly as such bequests are entirely exempt from capital transfer tax.

Widows Picking up one's life after the death of a spouse is often extremely hard, particularly for a young widow with chil-dren to support. The state provides a measure of help through benefits payable to widows and children, and there is also a special tax allowance called the *widow's bereavement allow-ance*, which, in the year of death and the following tax year, bridges the gap between the single and married personal allowance. This is on top of any entitlement to the additional personal allowance paid to single-parent families.

It is a pity that many people do not make a greater effort to leave their affairs in reasonable order. Making a will is one thing; setting out a list of personal information, including names, addresses and identification numbers of such things as banks, building societies, national savings, life assurance policies and the like, can save those who have to sort things out a great deal of unnecessary anxiety.

The financial consequences of divorce

In an ideal world, the likely financial arrangements on divorce would be codified, so a couple could work out in advance what their position would be in the event of their splitting up. Sadly this is not so. The fact is that with many divorces there is simply not enough money to go around; as a result, what seems fair to one party will be fiercely contested by the other. But what can you expect? The clearest starting point is the *one third rule*, which gives the former wife one third of the couple's joint income, and the husband two thirds. This proportion dates back to the time when wives were normally totally dependent on their husbands and, when divorced, took part of his earning power for support.

The law on divorce is being reformed but those who eagerly awaited new guidelines for maintenance payments were disappointed by the proposals. The only major change seemed to some to be rather peripheral: it denied the former non-working wife the absolute right to remain unemployed once the children were grown up. If she chooses not to work, the courts can impute an income to her before making any split of the husband's earnings.

In practice, though, the need to protect the lifestyle of the children overrides all other considerations in most marriages. Single-parent families are rapidly becoming the area of greatest financial deprivation in modern society; despite the fact that single parents get the married tax allowance and extra child benefit, they still prove the greatest claimants on the Welfare State. It is the ability of the father to pay that tends to dictate what the children will receive from a divorce settlement. At some levels school fees might be a possibility, while at others there is barely enough for school uniforms.

Maintenance   Each child has a tax-free allowance in his or her own right so it makes sense to direct maintenance to the child and save tax. Up to £33 a week counts as a *small maintenance payment* and can be paid over, gross, with no difficulties about reclaiming tax, so long as it is made under a court order.

Maintenance to the wife can be tax-deductible as long as it is in a legally binding form – which may mean no more than that she has good cause to rely on it. It is, though, taxable in her hands. Again, up to £33 a week can be received gross, tax being payable only if her other non-taxed income uses up her single person's allowance plus the additional tax allowance for children, if any. Above that, the husband deducts basic-rate tax at source and the wife has to reclaim any over-deduction. With small maintenance payments and for higher-rate tax, the husband has to reclaim tax through the coding system – a cumbersome exercise which rarely produces exactly the right figure for tax relief, bearing in mind that maintenance payments are fully tax-deductible.

Asset distribution   If the rules on maintenance out of income are unclear, asset distribution is even more so. For most couples there is only one asset, and that is a mortgaged house. It is very likely that the wife will be allowed to live there while the children are young, with some arrangement for it to be sold and the proceeds divided at a later date. Broadly, a wife can expect a half-share of assets acquired during the marriage and where the children are grown up, that often means selling the family home and dividing the proceeds to enable both parties to start again in something more modest.

Second marriages   As long as the divorced wife is being paid regular maintenance, she has the right to return to the courts for more if her husband's circumstances improve. This gives many ex-husbands a feeling of being hounded and puts a blight on many a second marriage. The new wife feels she is forced to go out to work and cannot afford children, while knowing the first wife will come back for more money the moment her ex-husband gets a pay rise or promotion. One way round this is to go for a *capital-only pay-off*. For many families, the only way this is possible is to allow the first wife to be given the whole of the marital home.

Pension rights   The pension is one asset, though, where the new wife does tend to take precedence. Most occupational schemes have no capacity to care for two dependants on death in retirement, so the second wife may get all the widow's rights. The loss of the right to be a man's widow is something a middle-aged wife should think carefully about while making her financial demands at divorce.

Under the state system it is more straightforward. As long as the ex-wife begins to contribute to her state retirement pension once the decree has been made absolute, she will get a full pension at 60 based on her husband's record to the date of divorce and her own thereafter.

Once the wife has secured her financial freedom, she will have some resources of her own; until that time, she may be penniless. In that event, she may claim legal aid on her divorce proceedings, but there is an obligation to repay the costs once the finances are finalized, unless, of course, the court deems them to be payable by the husband.

Remember there are no rules on financial settlements. Most maintenance ceases if a divorced woman remarries or, indeed, cohabits. There is little case law yet where the wife is the main breadwinner but certainly in the United States it is increasingly common for a man to sue his ex-wife for alimony. Overall, few couples survive divorce without considerable financial traumas.

Redundancy and coping with unemployment

The three million or so unemployed fall into three main groups. First, there are those who are temporarily out of work and hope to find another job within a matter of months. When they do, they will be replaced by yet more unemployed and to this extent the overall figures for those out of work give little more than a hint of the number of people who have lost their jobs in the last few years.

The second group covers those whose job prospects are poor, and who will have to rely on state benefits for support. It also includes a few of the wives who had hoped to work as joint breadwinners but who cannot get well-paid employment because of the prolonged recession. *Supplementary benefit* is available for anyone whose savings have run below £3,000 (plus £1,500 of surrender value of life policies). The rules are complex and a special subject in themselves, but there is no harm to be gained in applying for benefits. If you feel wronged, turn to the books published by the Child Poverty Action Group, who set out both means-tested and non-means-tested benefits in great detail.

The third group includes the increasing number of people who have been tempted by special payments or pension supplements to apply for early retirement. Over the age of 60, they no longer receive full unemployment benefit if their occupational pensions are worth more than £35 a week. (Benefit is lost pound for pound from this point, so a company pension of £78.85 is sufficient to wipe out the whole of a married man's unemployment benefit.) They also do not have to sign on to get outstanding national insurance contributions credited. As a result there may be many more people giving up work in their early sixties than the statistics suggest. Indeed, early retirement is something that many of us should expect in the future and hopefully pension entitlements from jobs will improve to allow for the fact that our working lives are likely to be shorter than they are now.

Redundancy If you are forced to leave your job through compulsory redundancy, you may have to take what you are given. At the moment, however, many redundancy pro-grammes are voluntary, so what factors should you consider if you are offered the chance of giving up work? The first is your pension. Some pension schemes will begin to pay out an early pension for men over the age of 55 (or even in some cases 50) but it may be severely reduced because it is to be paid for that much longer. Never volunteer for early retirement until you have seen in writing the impact that it will have on your pension expectations. Younger workers will have little choice initially but to leave their pensions behind, often in a frozen form. The government is planning to step in and force some increases but that will not apply retrospectively – only to service after the law is changed.

There are two other pension options that must be con-sidered. One is to uplift the transfer value and pay it into a fund designed for this purpose known as a *transplan vehicle* and run by an insurance company. Unless your service is quite long, and you have been earning well over the £10,000–£12,000 a year threshold for the guaranteed minimum pension, you may find there is little left for investment. The other option is to transfer your pension rights to your new employer when you get another job. You will almost certainly be disappointed in the offer of added years, but the blame lies with your former employer's scheme, not your new one. Above all, try to under-stand as clearly as possible what choices you have and where you will simply have to grin and bear it.

Lump-sum payments You may, of course, get a golden handshake or, at least, pay in lieu of notice. A lump-sum termination payment is tax-free up to £25,000 these days. On the next £25,000, you pay at half the rate you would have paid had you earned the money, three quarters on the next £25,000; only when the payment exceeds £75,000 is the top part of the golden handshake taxed in full as earned income. If you do run into tax difficulties, get help; for example, ask whether your previous employer could divert some of the money into extra pension, instead of giving it to you as a taxable lump sum.

Unemployment benefit   Unemployment benefit is now taxable and as it almost exactly equals the basic tax-free entitlement for a single or married person each week, it means that there is little chance of a tax refund from over-deduction on PAYE. In the past the refund was very useful to tide you over a short period of unemployment. Benefit is paid only once your period of notice has expired and then lasts for just 12 months, after which the only state help available is means-tested supplementary and housing benefits. As long as you are on some form of state benefit, your national insurance contributions will be credited to keep your track record up for state pension. If not (and you are under the age of 60), you must be prepared to make voluntary Class 3 contributions (£4.50 a week) for any year where your earnings fall below some £1,800. Check at the end of any financial year during which you have been out of work (say at the end of March) that your contributions record is adequate, and to be on the safe side ask for a written statement.

Taxing the unemployed   Your tax position, both short-term and long, will affect any decisions about investment. For non-taxpayers, stick with National Savings – the investment account (INVAC) and the income bond are good basics. Taxpayers should look first to the building societies and find those that pay over the odds to larger investors and who will pay you a monthly income, if you need it. But do not be tempted to lock your money up unless your plans are quite clear.

Paying off your mortgage   If redundancy is effectively early retirement, do think of paying off your mortgage. One less debt hanging over you will clear your mind and make your finances easier to manage but, if unemployment is likely to be temporary, hold on for a bit. Once paid off, you cannot get your mortgage back with tax relief unless you move. If losing your job comes as a shock, go to the building society and set your cards on the table. They can help; sadly, these days they have quite a bit of experience in redundancy counselling.

Investing a lump sum   If you have quite a bit of money to invest, settle down and develop your own expertise. A few benevolent employers send staff to independent financial advisers if they lose their jobs. Otherwise, treat with care anyone who purports to tell you what to do; he may be a commission salesman or simply a kindly know-all.

Remember you may have lost quite a bit more than simply your job. Even on slender resources, make sure as first priority that you have spent a bit of money on basic insurance to protect what you have, and, above all, do not be rushed into making decisions about moving house or investment. A little time spent thinking will never come amiss.

Setting up in business   At a time when there are three million unemployed, going it alone in your own business may seem an attractive proposition. If you have lost your job through no fault of your own, you may be able to capitalize on existing skills with a lump sum pay-off to use as working capital. It is fine in theory but it may not work out in practice for fundamental reasons, like having the wrong temperament, not enough self-discipline, commitment or confidence, quite apart from not having enough money.

There is no shortage of help or guidance available to budding entrepreneurs, not least a whole stack of books on the subject; this means that the first profitable move is to visit your local library. The Department of Industry has a series of booklets ranging from *Raising Finance* to *Moving Location* and from *Entering the Hotel and Catering Industry* to *Credit Control for Retailers*. There are departments in many of the larger town halls to help small businesses and two of the better-known trade organizations are The National Federation of the Self-Employed and Small Businesses and The Alliance of Small Firms and Self-Employed People.

It goes without saying that you must have a good idea to develop and there must be a viable market place for it, a gap you can profitably fill, whether it is manufacturing or providing a service. Thorough research pays dividends at every stage.

Assuming that you propose to operate a full-time business rather than earning some part-time money, then one of the earliest decisions you will have to make is whether to operate as a sole trader, in a partnership, or through a company (which can easily be bought 'off the peg' for about £100). Now that the government has reduced corporation tax for small companies, with profits under £100,000 a year, to 30 per cent, which is the same as basic-rate tax, there is an added incentive to turn a small firm into a limited company.

The sole trader   As a self-employed sole trader you have certain tax advantages, such as being able to offset start-up costs against previous years' earnings as an employee. You may also be able to base the first 2 or 3 years' tax assessments on the profits (or losses) of the opening year – which can start on any date of your own choosing. A self-employed person does not have to file audited accounts at Companies House. However, you will be liable for all your debts and your personal assets are taken to be part of the business.

Partnerships   Partnerships are simple to set up; partners are simply two or more self-employed people sharing. The distribution of profits can be valued to suit the individuals' needs and a husband and wife can use it for tax planning. When partnerships break down, however, there can be complications over the precise division of assets and profits.

Limited liability   With a limited liability company the directors stand to lose only the capital they have put up, apart from what is covered by any personal guarantees they may have given. In return they will have to comply with a great many complicated statutory provisions; an accountant and a solicitor are essential and should be sought out at the earliest opportunity, together with a friendly bank manager. This is not to say that a self-employed person can do without any of these, but he may be able to get started with much less in the way of formalities. You should never forget, however, that there will be a number of people breathing down your neck, not least the Inland Revenue, and (assuming your turnover is more than £18,700 a year or £6,200 a quarter) the Customs and Excise with whom you will have to register for VAT.

Initial finance   If you have been made redundant, it may be that you have received a lump sum which can be used to provide the initial finance, to rent premises, to buy the necessary tools and pay for services, heat, light, and so on, as well as lay in a stock of raw materials. If you consider buying into a franchise (the right to distribute or manufacture something or operate a service in a particular area, such as photocopying or fast food, under a nationally advertised brand name), make sure you understand precisely what you are getting for what is likely to be a substantial outlay. Check with the British Franchise

Association that the operation has a good track record and have your solicitor go minutely through the agreement.

Additional capital It is unlikely, however, that any business – or at least any successful and expanding business – can survive long without additional capital backing, and going round trying to raise money can be a very frustrating experience. People who lend money want to see solid evidence of achievement; enthusiasm is not enough. A bank – and that is where you will almost certainly start – will not be impressed by random jottings on the backs of envelopes. The bank manager will want a well thought out presentation with details of budgeting, pricing, marketing, projections of cash flow and estimates of future profitability, and the better you present your case, the more likely the bank is to back you, though it is quite likely to want collateral for a loan in the shape of a charge against existing investments or property. There is also the Business Expansion Scheme which enables individuals (though not the owners) to obtain full tax relief on investment up to £40,000 a year, subject to various restrictions which are outlined in Chapter 5.

The Loan Guarantee Scheme Obviously the more substantial the enterprise the greater the need for adequate capital and an overdraft from the bank may not be the answer. In fact, the government has given a considerable boost to smaller businesses through the Loan Guarantee Scheme, which enables them to borrow up to £75,000 from the banks without collateral, and the take-up of funds so far indicates this is a popular form of raising money.

APPENDIX

List of Tables
PERSONAL TAX RATES, ALLOWANCES AND BENEFITS

PERSONAL TAX RATES, ALLOWANCES AND BENEFITS

1 Personal tax allowances	1983–84	1984–85
Single (and wife's earnings)	£1,785	£2,005
Married	£2,795	£3,155
Single parent addition	£1,010	£1,150
Widow's bereavement	£1,010	£1,150
Age allowance (from age 65)		
Single	£2,360	£2,490
Married	£3,755	£3,955

Note Age allowance is clawed back £2 for every £3 of income when total income exceeds: £7,600 (1983–84); £8,100 (1984–85)

Dependent relative relief		
Single woman claimant	£145	£145
Others	£100	£100
Mortgage interest relief	£30,000 max.	£30,000 max.
Life assurance premium relief	15% tax relief on premiums £1,500 limit (or ⅙ of total income)	abolished for policies taken out after 13.3.84
Business Expansion Scheme Relief	£40,000 max.	£40,000 max.

Income tax rates	1983–84	%	1984–85	%
Basic rate	£1–14,600	30	£1–15,400	30
	£14,601–17,200	40	£15,401–18,200	40
	£17,201–21,800	45	£18,201–23,100	45
	£21,801–28,900	50	£23,101–30,600	50
	£28,901–36,000	55	£30,601–38,100	55
	£36,001 and above	60	£38,101 and above	60

Investment income surcharge

| Additional rate | £7,100 and above | 15 | abolished from 6.4.84 | |

Election for separate taxation (wife's earnings minimum)

| | £22,067 (£5,682) | | £23,794 (£6,389) | |

2 Capital gains tax: 30 per cent of net gains (after deducting annual exemption)

	1983–84	1984–85
Annual exemption	£5,300	£5,600
Chattels exemption	£3,000 (proceeds per item)	£3,000 (proceeds per item)

Note *Indexation applies to disposals (from 6 April 1982) and allows the cost of an asset to be increased by the increase in the Retail Prices Index, excluding the first year of ownership.*

| Retirement relief (on chargeable business assets) | £100,000 max. | £100,000 max. |

PERSONAL TAX RATES, ALLOWANCES AND BENEFITS

3 Capital transfer tax

Lifetime gifts (subject to donor surviving 3 years)

1983-84 bands	%	Cumulative tax	1984-85 bands	%	Cumulative tax
£0-60,000	nil	nil	£0-64,000	nil	nil
£60,001-80,000	15	£3,000	£64,001-85,000	15	£3,150
£80,001-110,000	17½	£8,250	£85,001-116,000	17½	£8,575
£110,001-140,000	20	£14,250	£116,001-148,000	20	£14,975
£140,001-175,000	22½	£22,125	£148,001-185,000	22½	£23,300
£175,001-220,000	25	£33,375	£185,001-232,000	25	£35,050
£220,001-270,000	30	£48,375	£232,001-285,000	27½	£49,625
£270,001-700,000	35	£198,875	£285,000 and above	30	
£700,001-1,325,000	40	£448,875			
£1,325,001-2,650,000	45	£1,045,125			
£2,650,000 and above	50				

Note Any lifetime gift drops out of the reckoning 10 years after it took place so the exercise can be repeated every 10 years.

Transfers at death (or within 3 years before)

1983–84 bands	%	Cumulative tax	1984–85 bands	%	Cumulative tax
£0–60,000	nil	nil	£0–64,000	nil	nil
£60,001–80,000	30	£6,000	£64,001–85,000	30	£6,300
£80,001–110,000	35	£16,500	£85,001–116,000	35	£17,150
£110,001–140,000	40	£28,500	£116,001–148,000	40	£29,950
£140,001–175,000	45	£44,250	£148,001–185,000	45	£46,600
£175,001–220,000	50	£66,750	£185,001–232,000	50	£70,100
£220,001–270,000	55	£94,250	£232,001–285,000	55	£99,250
£270,001–700,000	60	£352,250	£285,000 and above	60	
£700,001–1,325,000	65	£758,500			
£1,325,001–2,650,000	70	£1,686,000			
£2,650,000 and above	75				
Annual exemption		£3,000			£3,000
Small gifts		£250			£250
Gifts on marriage: From parent		£5,000			£5,000
From other relative or grandparent		£2,500			£2,500
From any other person		£1,000			£1,000
Charities		unlimited			unlimited

PERSONAL TAX RATES, ALLOWANCES AND BENEFITS

4 Fringe benefits

Motor cars

The amount of tax an employee pays is calculated by reference to scale rates of 'value'. The main car scale benefits for cars less than four years old (more than four years old in brackets) are as follows:

	1983–84	1984–85	1985–86
Up to 1300 cc	£325 (£225)	£375 (£250)	£410 (£275)
1301 to 1800 cc	£425 (£300)	£480 (£320)	£525 (£350)
Over 1800 cc	£650 (£450)	£750 (£500)	£825 (£550)
Original market value			
£14,001–£21,000	£950 (£650)		
£16,001–£24,000		£1,100 (£740)	
£17,501–£26,500			£1,200 (£800)
More expensive	£1,500 (£1,000)	£1,725 (£1,150)	£1,900 (£1,270)

Fuel benefits

Up to 1300 cc	£325	£375	£410
1301 to 1800 cc	£425	£480	£525
Over 1800 cc	£650	£750	£825

Note *Above rates are reduced by a half if business mileage is more than 18,000 miles in the fiscal year. Motor car benefits (but not petrol) are increased by half if business mileage is less than 2,500 miles in the fiscal year.*

5 Retirement annuity premium limits: self-employed pensions (SEDAs), including those in non-pensionable employment

1983–84		1984–85	
Year of birth	%	Year of birth	%
1934 or later	17½	1934 or later	17½
1916–1933	20	1916–1933	20
1914–1915	21	1914–1915	21
1912–1913	24	1912–1913	24
1910–1911	26½	1910–1911	26½
1908–1909	29½	1908–1909	29½
earlier (if below age 75)	32½		

PERSONAL TAX RATES, ALLOWANCES AND BENEFITS

6 National insurance contributions

	1983–84		1984–85	
Class 1: employed (per week)	**Earnings limits**	**%**	**Earnings limits**	**%**
Not contracted out				
Employee	£32.50–235	9	£34–250	9
Employer	£32.50–235	11.45	£34–250	11.45
Contracted out				
Employee	first £32.50	9	first £34	9
Employer	first £32.50	11.45	first £34	11.45
Employee	up to £235	6.85	up to £250	6.85
Employer	up to £235	7.35	up to £250	7.35
Married women/widows reduced rate		3.85		3.85
Class 2: self-employed flat weekly rate	£4.40		£4.60	
Lower earnings limit p.a.	£1,775		£1,850	
Class 3: non-employed weekly rate	£4.30		£4.50	
Class 4: self-employed assessable profits rate	£3,800–12,000	6.3	£3,950–13,000	6.3

7 State benefits (per week)	Up to 20 Nov 83	From 21 Nov 83	From 19 Nov 84
Retirement pension			
Single	£32.85	£34.05	
Married couple	£52.55	£54.50	

Note Total pension in tax year 1983–84 was: single £1,731; married couple £2,770. Widow's pension after first 26 weeks equals single retirement pension.

	Up to 20 Nov 83	From 21 Nov 83	From 19 Nov 84
Earnings limit for pensioners	£57.00	£65.00	
Child benefit	£5.85	£6.50	
One-parent benefit (first child)	£3.65	£4.05	
Invalidity pension (standard rate)			
Single	£31.45	£32.60	
Married	£50.30	£52.15	
Unemployment benefit			
Single	£25.00	£27.05	
Married	£40.45	£43.75	

Note To calculate amount for 1984—85 when rates are announced, multiply existing amount by 33 and new figure (from November 1984) by 19 (these being number of weeks in tax year for which respective amounts are paid).

163

PERSONAL TAX RATES, ALLOWANCES AND BENEFITS

State benefits (per week)	Up to 20 Nov 83	From 21 Nov 83	From 19 Nov 84
Sickness benefit			
Single	£25.00	£25.95	
Married	£40.45	£41.95	
Widow's allowance (first 26 weeks)	£45.95	£47.65	
Maternity allowance	£25.00	£25.95	
Attendance allowance			
Higher rate	£26.25	£27.20	
Lower rate	£17.50	£18.15	
Mobility allowance	£18.30	£19.00	
Therapeutic earnings limit	£20.00	£22.50	
Supplementary benefit (long-term)			
Single	£32.70	£34.10	
Married	£52.30	£54.55	

Supplementary benefit (short-term)

Single	£25.70	£26.80
Married	£41.70	£43.50

Capital cut-off (supp. benefit)

	£2,500	£3,000
Plus life insurance	nil	£1,500

Family income supplement

Income for family with one child below which FIS is payable	£82.50	£85.50
Each additional child	£9.00	£9.50
Weekly amount for one-child family	£21.00 max.	£22.00 max.

Note *The main statement on benefits uprating for 1984–85 is expected in June 1984. It will be based on the May Retail Prices Index and has been estimated at about 5½%.*

HOUSING

8 Building societies ranking by asset size

Company	Total assets at end 1983	Company	Total assets at end 1983
1 Halifax	£16,780m	11 Britannia	£2,376m
2 Abbey National	£14,313m	12 Cheltenham & Gloucester	£2,041m
3 Nationwide	£7,349m	13 Bristol & West	£1,574m
4 Leeds Permanent	£5,075m	14 Yorkshire	£1,214m
5 Woolwich	£4,850m	15 Gateway	£1,138m
6 National & Provincial	£3,917m	16 Northern Rock	£1,063m
7 Anglia	£3,653m	17 The Midshires	£677m
8 Alliance	£2,791m	18 The Town and Country	£638m
9 Bradford & Bingley	£2,687m	19 The Coventry	£572m
10 Leicester	£2,477m	20 The Guardian	£569m

9 Monthly net repayments on a £10,000 loan with Mortgage Interest Relief at Source

Gross mortgage rate %	20-year term	25-year term	30-year term
9.00	£74.50	£67.10	£62.50
9.25	£75.55	£68.25	£63.70
9.50	£76.60	£69.30	£64.90
9.75	£77.65	£70.45	£66.05
10.00	£78.70	£71.60	£67.20
10.25	**£79.75**	**£72.70**	**£68.40**
10.50	£80.90	£73.80	£69.60
10.75	£81.95	£74.95	£70.80
11.00	£83.00	£76.10	£72.00
11.25	£84.15	£77.25	£73.20
11.50	£85.20	£78.40	£74.40
11.75	£86.35	£79.65	£75.65
12.00	£87.50	£80.80	£76.90
12.25	£88.60	£82.00	£78.10
12.50	£89.70	£83.20	£79.40

Note *The advised mortgage rate in spring 1984 is 10.25 per cent.*

HOUSING

10 Advance of £10,000 repayable over 25 years at 10.25 per cent gross (7.175 per cent net under MIRAS system)

Year	Constant net annual repayment	Principal	Interest	Balance at end of year
1	£874.80	£157.30	£717.50	£9,842.70
2	£874.80	£168.59	£706.21	£9,674.11
3	£874.80	£180.68	£694.12	£9,493.43
4	£874.80	£193.65	£681.15	£9,299.78
5	£874.80	£207.54	£667.26	£9,092.24
6	£874.80	£222.43	£652.37	£8,869.81
7	£874.80	£238.39	£636.41	£8,631.42
8	£874.80	£255.50	£619.30	£8,375.92
9	£874.80	£273.83	£600.97	£8,102.09
10	£874.80	£293.48	£581.32	£7,808.61
11	£874.80	£314.53	£560.27	£7,494.08
12	£874.80	£337.10	£537.70	£7,156.98

13	£874.80	£361.29	£513.51	£6,795.69
14	£874.80	£387.21	£487.59	£6,408.48
15	£874.80	£414.99	£459.81	£5,993.49
16	£874.80	£444.77	£430.03	£5,548.72
17	£874.80	£476.68	£398.12	£5,072.04
18	£874.80	£510.88	£363.92	£4,561.16
19	£874.80	£547.54	£327.26	£4,013.62
20	£874.80	£586.82	£287.98	£3,426.80
21	£874.80	£628.93	£245.87	£2,797.87
22	£874.80	£674.05	£200.75	£2,123.82
23	£874.80	£722.42	£152.38	£1,401.40
24	£874.80	£774.25	£100.55	£627.15
25	£672.15	£672.15	£45.00	–
Total	**£21,667.35**	**£10,000.00**	**£11,667.35**	

Note *Calculations assume annual intervals and no changes in the interest rate payable or in the basic rate of income tax. Tax relief is at the basic rate of 30%.*

Courtesy: Building Societies Association

HOUSING

11 Building society mortgage rate and ordinary share rate comparisons

Date	Mortgage rate %	Share rate (net) %	Share rate (gross) %
1 January 1980	15.00	10.50	15.00
1 January 1981	14.00	9.25	13.21
1 April 1981	13.00	8.50	12.14
1 November 1981	15.00	9.75	13.93
1 April 1982	13.50	8.75	12.50
1 September 1982	12.00	7.75	11.07
1 December 1982	10.00	6.25	8.93
1 July 1983	11.25	7.25	10.36
1 April 1984	10.25	6.25	8.93

Note *In 1983 the Building Societies Association decided to scrap the 'recommended' rate in favour of the 'advised' rate.*

12 Bank base rates of interest

Date	Base rate %	7-day deposit %
25 January 1982	14	11½

Date		
25 February 1982	13½	11
12 March 1982	13	10
9 June 1982	12½	9½
14 July 1982	12	9
2 August 1982	11½	8½
18 August 1982	11	8
31 August 1982	10½	7¼
7 October 1982	10	6¾
14 October 1982	9½	6
5 November 1982	9	5½
29 November 1982	10	6¾
12 January 1983	11	8
15 March 1983	10½	7½
15 April 1983	10	6¾
15 June 1983	9½	6
3 October 1983	9	5½
15 March 1984	8½	5¼

HOUSING

13 House rebuilding cost index per sq ft for insurance House contents valuation index

July 1978	100.0	July 1978	181.8
September 1978	102.1	September 1978	184.9
March 1979	108.5	March 1979	191.8
September 1979	124.9	September 1979	210.6
March 1980	130.7	March 1980	223.1
September 1980	143.8	September 1980	229.2
March 1981	146.8	March 1981	234.9
September 1981	149.3	September 1981	240.6
March 1982	152.9	March 1982	242.8
September 1982	161.5	September 1982	245.0
March 1983	164.5	March 1983	249.3
September 1983	170.7	September 1983	251.6
March 1984	173.7	March 1984	255.6

Note *These tables determine the increase in the cost of rebuilding or in the value of durable household goods. Apply the rebuilding index to a home which cost £40,000 to rebuild in March 1983 and there will be an increase of just over £2,000 by March 1984.*

14 Stamp duty on transfers of property

1983–84	%	1984–85	%
£0–25,000	nil		
£25,001–30,000	½	£0–30,000	nil
£30,001–35,000	1	£30,001 and above	1
£35,001–40,000	1½		
£40,001 and above	2		

Note *No tapering of the new flat 1% rate: a transfer of £30,000 attracts no stamp duty and a transfer of £30,001 costs £300.*

15 Land registry fees

Sample purchase price	First registration	Subsequent registrations
£14,000	£21	£33
£16,000	£24	£38
£18,000	£27	£43
£20,000	£30	£48
£25,000	£39	£63
£30,000	£45	£73
£35,000	£54	£83
£40,000	£60	£98

INVESTMENT PERFORMANCE

16 *Financial Times* Ordinary Share Index (for year ending)

1974	161.4	1979	414.2
1975	375.7	1980	474.5
1976	354.7	1981	530.4
1977	485.4	1982	593.6
1978	470.9	1983	775.7

Note The low point of the decade – 146 – was reached on 6 January 1975.

17 Best-performing unit trusts to end of 1983: £1,000 invested

1 year

1 GT European	£1,984
2 Abbey Japan	£1,925
3 Fidelity Japan	£1,832

3 years

1 Crescent Tokyo	£3,128
2 M & G American Recovery	£3,056
3 Oppenheimer International Growth	£2,964

4 Crescent Tokyo	£1,799
5 TSB Pacific	£1,762
6 HK Japan	£1,751
7 Henderson European	£1,747
8 Oppenheimer International Growth	£1,745
9 Aitken Hume Energy	£1,734
10 Tyndall Australian	£1,697

5 years

1 MLA Trust	£4,800
2 Oppenheimer International Growth	£4,387
3 GT US & General	£4,245
4 Britannia American Smaller Co's	£4,193
5 Henderson American Smaller Co's	£4,190
6 Arbuthnot Foreign	£4,162
7 Britannia Gold & General	£4,158
8 Framlington American General	£3,892
9 Bishopsgate International	£3,857
10 Framlington International	£3,834

4 Arbuthnot Foreign	£2,744
5 Arbuthnot Smaller Co's	£2,695
6 Target Gold Fund	£2,684
7 Hill Samuel Far East	£2,682
8 Framlington American Turnaround	£2,679
9 MLA Trust	£2,635
10 Henderson Japan	£2,630

7 years

1 MLA Unit Trust	£9,930
2 Framlington International	£7,592
3 Britannia Smaller Co's	£6,989
4 Framlington Capital	£6,543
5 Allied Smaller Co's	£6,401
6 Aitken Hume Smaller Co's	£6,370
7 Leo Capital	£6,356
8 Henderson Capital	£6,254
9 M & G Recovery	£6,141
10 Allied Second Smaller Co's	£5,956

Courtesy: Money Management

INVESTMENT PERFORMANCE

18 Best-performing life insurance companies (with-profits endowment): gross premium of £10 per month maturing 1984

10-year term		15-year term	
1 Ecclesiastical	£2,263	1 Standard Life	£4,511
2 Equitable Life	£2,258	2 Norwich Union	£4,458
3 Standard Life	£2,255	3 Equitable Life	£4,391
4 Norwich Union	£2,249	4 Scottish Amicable	£4,317
5 Scottish Widows	£2,235	5 Ecclesiastical	£4,291
6 R.N.P.F.N.	£2,223	6 Scottish Widows	£4,245
7 Scottish Amicable	£2,197	7 UK Provident	£4,176
8 Scottish Mutual	£2,155	8 R.N.P.F.N.	£4,170
9 UK Provident	£2,137	9 Clerical, Medical & General	£4,136
10 Clerical, Medical & General	£2,136	10 Friends' Provident	£4,081

Courtesy: Money Management

19 Best-performing life insurance companies (unit-linked): gross premium of £20 per month maturing 1984

10-year term

1 Friends' Provident (Equity)	£7,866
2 Equitable (Pelican)	£7,152
3 S & P (US Growth)	£7,103
4 S & P (Japan Growth)	£6,787
5 British National (Framlington Capital)	£6,693
6 M & G (Recovery)	£6,450
7 M & G (Smaller Companies)	£6,180
8 S & P (Select International)	£6,109
9 London & Manchester (Investment Trusts)	£6,100
10 Norwich Union	£6,089

15-year term

1 British National (Framlington Capital)	£14,145
2 M & G (Smaller Companies)	£12,061
3 M & G (Dividend)	£11,812
4 Scottish Widows	£11,789
5 Norwich Union	£11,454
6 Barclays (Income)	£11,394
7 M & G (Second General)	£11,335
8 Barclays (500)	£11,004
9 Barclays (General)	£10,806
10 M & G (Midland & General)	£10,666

Note *Because unit-linked funds are of much more recent origin the above tables do not reflect the great diversity of plans now available in the market.*

Courtesy: *Planned Savings*

INVESTMENT PERFORMANCE

20 Unit trust performance

Current value of £1,000 (as at 1 January 1984) invested 5, 10 or 15 years ago, with net income reinvested

	General	Growth	Equity income	N. American	Far Eastern
5 years	£2,247	£2,271	£1,984	£2,724	£2,316
No. of funds in sector	73	55	68	28	21
10 years	£4,166	£3,942	£4,255	£3,075	£3,398
No. of funds in sector	57	45	42	14	11
15 years	£3,884	£4,204	£4,486	£2,685	£2,980
No. of funds in sector	32	17	19	5	1

	European	International	Commodity & Energy	Financial & Property	Investment Trust units
5 years	£1,737	£2,448	£2,169	£2,447	£2,593
No. of funds in sector	5	39	17	12	7
10 years	£2,850	£3,478	£3,822	£3,164	£4,820
No. of funds in sector	4	29	11	11	6

15 years	£2,861	£3,410	£4,316	£3,754	£3,289
No. of funds in sector	1	11	8	6	4

	Preference Share units	Gilt & Fixed Interest growth	Gilt & Fixed Interest income	Income (Mixed/Pref/Equity)
5 years	£1,410	£1,566	£1,613	£1,735
No. of funds in sector	6	1	2	2
10 years	£2,633	–	–	£3,625
No. of funds in sector	3	–	–	9
15 years	£2,242	–	–	£3,397
No. of funds in sector	1	–	–	3

Comparative note: figures assume net income reinvested

	Financial Times 30 Index	Bank deposit account	Building society ordinary share account
5 years	£2,034	£1,433	£1,526
10 years	£3,446	£1,794	£2,149
15 years	£2,659	£2,141	£2,785

Courtesy: Unit Trust Association, January 1984

INFLATION

21 Retail Prices Index: monthly average 1962–84

Year	Jan.	Feb.	Mar.	Apr.	May	Jun.	Jul.	Aug.	Sep.	Oct.	Nov.	Dec.
1962	52.1	52.2	52.4	53.1	53.3	53.6	53.4	53.0	52.9	52.9	53.1	53.3
1963	53.5	54.0	54.1	54.2	54.2	54.2	53.9	53.7	53.9	54.1	54.2	54.3
1964	54.6	54.6	54.8	55.3	55.8	56.0	56.0	56.2	56.2	56.3	56.7	56.9
1965	57.1	57.1	57.3	58.4	58.6	58.8	58.8	58.9	58.9	59.0	59.2	59.5
1966	59.6	59.6	59.7	60.5	60.9	61.1	60.8	61.2	61.1	61.2	61.6	61.7
1967	61.8	61.8	61.8	62.3	62.3	62.5	62.1	62.0	61.9	62.4	62.8	63.2
1968	63.4	63.7	63.9	65.1	65.1	65.4	65.4	65.5	65.6	65.9	66.1	66.9
1969	67.3	67.7	67.9	68.7	68.6	68.9	68.9	68.7	68.9	69.4	69.6	70.1
1970	70.6	71.0	71.4	72.5	72.7	72.9	73.5	73.4	73.8	74.6	75.1	75.6
1971	76.6	77.1	77.7	79.4	79.9	80.4	80.9	81.0	81.1	81.5	82.0	82.4
1972	82.9	83.3	83.6	84.4	84.8	85.3	85.6	86.3	86.8	88.0	88.3	88.7
1973	89.3	89.9	90.4	92.1	92.8	93.3	93.7	94.0	94.8	96.7	97.4	98.1
1974	100.0	101.7	102.6	106.1	107.6	108.7	109.7	109.8	111.0	113.2	115.2	116.9

Year												
1975	119.9	121.9	124.3	129.1	134.5	137.1	138.5	139.3	140.5	142.5	144.2	146.0
1976	147.9	149.8	150.6	153.5	155.2	156.0	156.3	158.5	160.6	163.5	165.8	168.0
1977	172.4	174.1	175.8	180.3	181.7	183.6	183.8	184.7	185.7	186.5	187.4	188.4
1978	189.5	190.6	191.8	194.6	195.7	197.2	198.1	199.4	200.2	201.1	202.5	204.2
1979	207.2	208.9	210.6	214.2	215.9	219.6	229.1	230.9	233.2	235.6	237.7	239.4
1980	245.3	248.8	252.2	260.8	263.2	265.7	267.9	268.5	270.2	271.9	274.1	275.6
1981	277.3	279.8	284.0	292.2	294.1	295.8	297.1	299.3	301.0	303.7	306.9	308.8
1982	310.6	310.7	313.4	319.7	322.0	322.9	323.0	323.1	322.9	324.5	326.1	325.5
1983	325.9	327.3	327.9	332.5	333.9	334.7	336.5	338.0	339.5	340.7	341.9	342.8
1984	342.6	344.0	345.1									

Note *The index was established at 100 in January 1974.*

Courtesy: Central Statistical Office

181

INFLATION

22 Retail Price Index: annual average 1914–83

Year	Average	Year	Average	Year	Average	Year	Average	Year	Average
1914	11.1	1927	18.7	1946	29.4	1959	49.1	1972	85.7
1915	13.7	1928	18.5	1947	31.4	1960	49.6	1973	93.5
1916	16.2	1929	18.2	1948	33.8	1961	51.0	1974	108.5
1917	19.6	1930	17.6	1949	34.6	1962	53.0	1975	134.8
1918	22.6	1931	16.4	1950	35.6	1963	54.0	1976	157.1
1919	23.9	1932	16.0	1951	38.8	1964	55.8	1977	182.0
1920	27.7	1933	15.6	1952	41.2	1965	58.4	1978	197.1
1921	25.1	1934	15.7	1953	41.9	1966	60.7	1979	223.5
1922	20.4	1935	15.9	1954	42.6	1967	62.3	1980	263.7
1923	19.4	1936	16.4	1955	44.1	1968	65.2	1981	295.0
1924	19.5	1937	17.2	1956	46.0	1969	68.7	1982	320.4
1925	19.6	1938	17.4	1957	47.5	1970	73.1	1983	335.1
1926	19.1	—	—	1958	48.8	1971	80.0		

Note There was no index in World War II.

Courtesy: Central Statistical Office

Organizations: Address List

Banking and building societies

Banking Information Service, 10 Lombard Street, London EC3V 9AR

Building Societies Association (BSA), 3 Savile Row, London W1X 1AF

Credit Union League of Great Britain Ltd, PO Box 135, Credit Union Centre, High Street, Skelmersdale, Lancs. WN8 8AP

Finance Houses Association, 18 Upper Grosvenor Street, London W1X 9PB

Friendly Societies Registry, 17 North Audley Street, London W1Y 2AP

National Conference of Friendly Societies, Victoria House, Vernon Place, London WC1B 4DP

National Federation of Credit Unions, The Cottage, 18 The Downs, London SW20 8HR

Charities

Charities Aid Foundation, 48 Pembury Road, Tonbridge, Kent TN9 2JD

Consumer affairs

Chartered Institute of Arbitrators, 75 Cannon Street, London EC4N 5BH

Consumers' Association, 14 Buckingham Street, London WC2N 6DS

National Association of Citizens' Advice Bureaux, 110 Drury Lane, London WC2B 5SU

National Consumer Council, 18 Queen Anne's Gate, London SW1H 9AA

National Federation of Consumer Groups, 12 Mosley Street, Newcastle upon Tyne NE1 1DE

Office of Fair Trading, Field House, 15–25 Bream's Buildings, London EC4A 1PR

Which? Publications, Consumers' Association, Castlemead, Gascoyne Way, Hertford SG14 1LH

Family and children

CRUSE, the National Organisation for the Widowed and their Children, 126 Sheen Road, Richmond, Surrey TW9 1UR

Gingerbread, an Association for One Parent Families Ltd, 35 Wellington Street, London WC2E 7BN

Maternity Alliance, 309 Kentish Town Road, London NW5 2TJ

National Association of Funeral Directors, 57 Doughty Street, London WC1N 2DE

National Association of Widows, Widows' Advisory Service, Chell Road, Stafford ST16 2QA

National Council for the Divorced and Separated, 13 High Street, Little Shelford, Cambridge CB2 5ES

National Council for One Parent Families, 255 Kentish Town Road, London NW5 2LX

National Council for the Single Woman and Her Dependants Ltd, 29 Chilworth Mews, London W2 3RG

Housing and property

British Association of Removers, 279 Gray's Inn Road, London WC1X 3SY

British Property Timeshare Association, Langham House, 308 Regent Street, London W1R 5AL

Building Centre, 26 Store Street, London WC1E 7BT

Federation of Private Residents' Association, 83 Cambridge Street, London SW1V 4PS

Householders' Association, The Computer Centre, 33 New Cavendish Street, London W1

Incorporated Society of Valuers & Auctioneers, 3 Cadogan Gate, London SW1X 0AS

Land Registry, 32 Lincoln's Inn Fields, London WC2A 3PH

National Association of Conveyancers, 2–4 Chichester Rents, London WC2A 1EJ

National Association of Estate Agents, 21 Jury Street, Warwick CV34 4EH

National Federation of Building Trades Employers, 18–20 Duchess Mews, London W1

National Federation of Housing Associations, 30–32 Southampton Street, London WC2E 7HE

National House Building Council, 58 Portland Place, London W1N 4BU

National Tenants Organisation, c/o National Consumer Council, 18 Queen Anne's Gate, London SW1H 9AA

Royal Incorporation of Architects in Scotland, 15 Rutland Square,

Edinburgh EH1 2HE

Royal Institute of British Architects (RIBA), 66 Portland Place, London W1N 4AD

Royal Institution of Chartered Surveyors (RICS), 12 Great George Street, London SW1P 3AD

SHAC (London Housing Aid Centre), 189a Old Brompton Road, London SW5 0AR

Shelter, 157 Waterloo Road, London SE1 8UU

Small Landlords' Association, 7 Rosedene Avenue, Streatham, London SW16 2JH

Insurance (life)

Association of British Travel Agents (ABTA), 55 Newman Street, London W1P 4AH

Association of Scottish Life Offices, 23 St Andrew's Square, Edinburgh 2

British Insurance Association, Aldermary House, 10–15 Queen Street, London EC4N 1TU

British Insurance Brokers' Association (BIBA), Fountain House, 130 Fenchurch Street, London EC3M 5DJ

Chartered Institute of Loss Adjusters, Manfield House, 376 Strand, London WC2R 0LR

Corporation of Insurance and Financial Advisers, 6–7 Leapale Road, Guildford, Surrey GU1 4JX

Institute of Public Loss Assessors, 14 Red Lion Street, Chesham, Bucks HP5 1HB

Insurance Brokers' Registration Council, 15 St Helen's Place, London EC3

Insurance Ombudsman Bureau, 31 Southampton Row, London WC1B 5HJ

Life Offices' Association, Aldermary House, 10–15 Queen Street, London EC4N 1TU

Linked Life Assurance Group, 12–16 Watling Street, London EC4M 9BB

Personal Insurance Arbitration Service (PIAS), c/o Chartered Institute of Arbitrators, International Arbitration Centre, 75 Cannon Street, London EC4N 5BH

Investment

Association of Independent Investment Managers, 19 Widegate Street, London E1 7HP

Association of Investment Trust Companies, Park House, 16 Finsbury Circus, London EC2M 7JJ

Chartered Institute of Public Finance and Accountancy (CIPFA) Loans Bureau, 232 Vauxhall Bridge Road, London SW1V 1AU

National Association of Investment Clubs, Halifax House, 5 Fenwick Street, Liverpool L2 0PR

National Association of Securities Dealers and Investment Managers (NASDIM), 27–28 Lovat Lane, London EC3R 8EB

Savers' Union, 3½ London Wall Buildings, London Wall, London EC2M 5SY

Unit Trust Association, Park House, 16 Finsbury Circus, London EC2M 7JP

Wider Share Ownership Council, Juxon House, 94 St Paul's Churchyard, London EC4M 8EH

Law

British Legal Association, 29 Church Road, Tunbridge Wells, Kent TN1 1HT

Law Society, 113 Chancery Lane, London WC2A 1PL

Law Society of Scotland, Law Society's Hall, 26 Drumsheugh Gardens, Edinburgh EH3 7YR

Legal Action Group, 28a Highgate Road, London NW5 1NS

National savings

Department of National Savings, Charles House, 375 Kensington High Street, London W14 8SD)

Pensions and retirement

Age Concern, Bernard Sunley House, 60 Pitcairn Road, Mitcham, Surrey CR4 3LL

Company Pensions Information Centre, 7 Old Park Lane, London W1Y 3LJ

Help the Aged, 32 Dover Street, London W1A 2AP

National Association of Pension Funds (NAPF), Sunley House, Bedford Park, Croydon, Surrey CR0 0XF

National Federation of Old Age
Pensions Associations (Pensioners'
Voice), Melling House, 91 Preston New
Road, Blackburn, Lancs. BB2 6BD
Occupational Pensions Advisory
Service, Room 327, Aviation House,
129 Kingsway, London WC2B 6NN
Pre-Retirement Association, 19 Undine
Street, Tooting, London SW17 8PP

Self-employed and small businesses
Alliance of Small Firms and Self-
Employed People Ltd, 42 Vine Street,
East Molesey, Surrey KT8 9LF
Association of British Chambers of
Commerce, 212 Shaftesbury Avenue,
London WC2H 8EB
British Franchise Association Ltd,
Grove House, 628 London Road,
Colnbrook, Slough, Berks. SL3 8QH
Council for Small Industries in Rural
Areas (CoSIRA), 141 Castle Street,
Salisbury, Wilts. SP1 1TP
National Federation of Self-Employed
and Small Businesses Ltd (NFSE), 32
St Anne's Road West, Lytham St
Annes, Lancs. FY8 1NY
Small Firms Information Service, Ebury
Bridge House, 2–18 Ebury Bridge
Road, London SW1W 8QD
Trades Union Congress, Congress
House, 23–28 Great Russell Street,
London WC1B 3LS

Social security
Child Poverty Action Group (CPAG),
1 Macklin Street, London WC2B 5NH
Department of Industry, Small Firms
Division, Ashdown House, 123 Victoria
Street, London SW1E 6RB
Dignity in Death Alliance, c/o Age
Concern, Bernard Sunley House, 60
Pitcairn Road, Mitcham, Surrey
CR4 3LL
Disability Alliance, 25 Denmark Street,
London WC2 8NJ
Royal Association for Disability and
Rehabilitation (RADAR), 25 Mortimer
Street, London W1N 8AB

Taxation
Association of Certified Accountants,
29 Lincoln's Inn Fields, London
WC2A 3EE
Capital Taxes Offices (England and
Wales), Minford House, Rockley Road,
London W14 0DF
Institute of Chartered Accountants in
England and Wales, PO Box 433,
Chartered Accountants' Hall,
Moorgate Place, London EC2P 2BJ
Institute of Chartered Accountants in-
Scotland, 27 Queen Street, Edinburgh
EH2 1LA
Probate Personal Application Dept,
Golden Cross House (5th floor),
Duncannon Street, London
WC2N 4JF
Tax Payers' Society, Room 22,
Wheatsheaf House, 4 Carmelite
Street, London EC4Y 0JA

Further Reading

Addresses of those organizations
marked with an asterisk can be found
under the appropriate group heading in
the Organizations Address List. Prices
and details were correct at time of going
to press, but do bear in mind that many
of these books will have to be revised
following the fundamental changes in
the 1984 Budget.

General
How to Survive Your Money Problems
Katherine Whitehorn (Methuen, 1983,
£3.95)
Money Book Margaret Allen (Pan, 2nd
edn, 1982, £2.95)
Trustee Savings Bank Money Guide
Marie Jennings (Collins, 1983, £2.50)
'Which?' Book of Money (Consumers'
Association* and Hodder, 1982, out of
print, £9.95)

Banking

Beat Your Bank Manager Wendy Elkington (Ward Lock, 1981, hbk £6.50, pbk £3.95)

How to Manage Your Bank Manager John Duncan (David & Charles, 1982, £3.95)

Commodities

Training in Commodities Ed. C.W.J. Granger (Woodhead-Faulkner, 4th edn, 1983, hbk £10.95, pbk £6.95)

Consumer affairs

Consumers: Know Your Rights John Harries (Oyez Longman, 3rd edn, 1983, £4.50)

Coping with the System Robert Leach (National Extension College, 1980, £2.50)

Handbook of Consumer Law (Consumers' Association,* 1982, £3.95)

'Which?' Guide to your Rights (Consumers' Association,* 1983, £4.95)

'Which?' Way to Complain (Consumers' Association* and Hodder, 1983, £4.95)

Family and children

Divorce and Your Money W.M. Harper (Unwin Paperbacks, 1981, £1.95)

How to Make Out a Deed of Covenant ⋅ Lourna Bourke (Bourke Publishers Ltd, PO Box 109, London SW5 9JP, 1983, £4.50)

How to Survive as a Second Wife Maggie Drummond (Robson Books, 1982, £2.95)

Living Together Clare Dyer, Marcel Berlins (Hamlyn, 1982, £1.50)

Money Matters for Women Liz McDonnell (Collins Willow, 1983, £2.95)

On Getting Divorced (Consumers' Association,* 1978, £4.95)

Women's Rights: A Practical Guide Anna Coote, Tess Gill (Penguin, 3rd edn, 1981, £3.95)

Your Children's Future (Legal & General, 2 Montefiore Road, Hove, East Sussex BM3 15E, 1983, free)

Housing and property

'Abbey National' Book of the Home Jill Blake (Octopus Books, 1982, £6.95)

Bradshaw's Guide to Do-it-Yourself Buying, Selling and Conveyancing Joseph Bradshaw (Castle Books Leamington Spa, rev. edn, 1983, hbk £8.45; pbk £5.45)

Other related titles by the same author published by Castle Books Leamington Spa: *Bradshaw's Guide to Conveyancing by Way of Gift and Inheritance* (1984, £4.45), *Bradshaw's Guide to House Conveyancing for Sitting Tenants* (1983, £3.00), *Bradshaw's Guide to Marketing Your House* (1983, £3.00)

Buying a House or Flat: Do's and Don'ts (Bedford Square Press, 5th edn, 1982, £1.50)

Buying and Moving House (Legal & General, 2 Montefiore Road, Hove, East Sussex BM3 1SE, 1983, free)

Buying and Selling a House or Flat Marjorie Giles (Pan, 2nd edn, 1981, £1.75)

Consumer's Guide to Mortgages Diana Wright (*Daily Telegraph*, 1983, £2.95)

Conveyancing Fraud, The Michael Joseph (M. Joseph, Woolwich, rev. edn, 1984, £3.95)

Rights Guide for Home Owners Janet Albeson and Lorna Gordon (SHAC, London Housing Aid Centre)* and Child Poverty Action Group,* rev. edn, 1983, £1.50)

'Which?' Way to Buy, Sell and Move House Ed. Edith Rudinger (Consumers' Association,* 1983, £6.95)

'Which?' Way to Cut Heating Bills (Consumers' Association* and Hodder, 1982, £6.95)

Insurance

Guide to Insurance Margaret Allen (Pan, 1982, £1.95)

Insurance Buyer's Guide Ed. Roger Anderson (Kluwer, 1984, £9.95)

Value for Money Insurance – What to Buy and How to Buy It (Flame Books, 1983, £2.95)

Insurance (life)

How to Plan Your Life Insurance Christopher Gilchrist (Martin Books, 1979, hbk £7.95, pbk £2.25)

Investment

Alternative Investment Robert Duthy (Michael Joseph, 1978, £8.50)

'Daily Mail' Money Mail Saver's Guide 1983–4 David Lewis (Harmsworth Publications, 1984, £1.25)

Guide to Savings and Investment James Rowlatt (Pan, 3rd edn, 1983, £2.50)

How to Invest Successfully Felicity Taylor (Kogan Page, 1983, hbk £8.95, pbk £4.95)

Investing for Beginners Daniel O'Shea (*Financial Times* Business Publishing, 1982, £7.50)

Investment Trusts Explained A.A. Arnaud (Woodhead-Faulkner, 1983, £6.95)

101 Ways of Investing and Saving Money (*Sunday Telegraph*, 1983, £1.95)

Perks from Shares: Guide to Shareholders' Concessions Alan Ramsey (Kogan Page, 1983, hbk £7.95, pbk £3.95)

Unit Trusts: What Every Investor Should Know Christopher Gilchrist (Woodhead-Faulkner, 3rd edn, 1982, hbk £9.95, pbk £6.25)

'Which?' Book of Saving and Investing (Consumers' Association* and Hodder, 1983, £10.95)

Your Taxes and Savings in Retirement Rosemary Burr (Age Concern,* 1983, £1.00 or £1.20 inc. p. and p.)

Jobs and redundancy

Coping with Redundancy Fred Kemp, Bernard Buttle, Derek Kemp (Hamlyn Paperbacks, 1982, £1.50)

Earning Money at Home (Consumers' Association,* 1982, £4.95)

How to Earn a Second Income Godfrey Golzen (Muller, 1983, £7.95)

How to Survive Unemployment: Creative Alternatives Robert Nathan, Michel Syrett (Penguin, 2nd edn, 1983, £2.95)

Jobs in a Jobless World: Where They Are and How to Get Them Godfrey Golzen (Muller, 1983, hbk £7.95, pbk £4.95)

Work for Yourself: A Guide for Young People Paddy Hall (National Extension College, 1983, £3.25)

Overseas working

Working Abroad Godfrey Golzen, Margaret Stewart (Kogan Page, 6th edn, 1983, hbk £9.95, pbk £5.95)

Working Abroad: An Expatriate's Guide David Young (*Financial Times* Business Publishing, 1983, £9.95)

Pensions

Self-Employed Pensions Ed. Janet Walford (*Financial Times* Business Publishing, 1983, £14.00)

Understanding Pension Schemes Maurice Oldfield (Fourmat Publishing, 1983, £7.95)

Retirement

Approaching Retirement (Consumers' Association* and Hodder, 1983, £4.95)

Focus on Retirement Fred Kemp, Bernard Buttle (Kogan Page, 1979, hbk £6.95, pbk £3.50)

Money and Your Retirement Edward Eves (Pre-Retirement Association,* 1984, £3.50)

Moving Home in Retirement? Lorna Gordon, Rose Moreno (SHAC, London Housing Aid Centre),* 1982, £0.85)

Planning for Your Retirement (Legal & General, 2 Montefiore Road, Hove, East Sussex BM3 1SE, 1984, free)

Retiring Abroad David Young (*Financial Times* Business Publishing, 1982, £8.50)

Your Holidays in Retirement Jane Minter, Sue Nicholson (Age Concern,* 1982, £0.70 or £0.90 inc. p. and p.)

Your Housing in Retirement Janice Casey (Age Concern,* 1983, £1.00 or £1.20 inc. p. and p.)

Your Pension (National Federation of Old Age Pensions Associations,* 1983–84, £0.75 inc. p. and p.)

Your Rights: For Pensioners (Age Concern,* 1983, £0.60 or £0.75 inc. p. and p.)

Your Taxes and Savings in Retirement (Age Concern,* 1983, £1.00 or £1.20 inc. p. and p.)

Self-employed and small businesses

'Guardian' Guide to Running a Small Business (Kogan Page, 1981, £4.25)

How to Set Up and Run Your Own Business (*Daily Telegraph*, 2nd edn, 1983, hbk £6.95, pbk £2.95)

How to Start and Run Your Own Business M. Mogano (Graham and Trotman, 4th edn, 1983, £3.95)

Small Business Guide: Sources of Information for New and Small Businesses Colin Barrow (BBC, 1982, £4.50)

Small Business Kit: Advice and Information on Starting or Buying a Business Ed. Woodcock (National Extension College, 2nd edn, 1981, £5.95)

Starting Your Own Business (Consumers' Association,* 1983, £4.95)

Taking Up a Franchise Godfrey Golzen (Kogan Page, 1983, hbk £11.95, pbk £5.95)

Working for Yourself: 'Daily Telegraph' Guide to Self Employment Godfrey Golzen (Kogan Page, 6th edn, 1983, hbk £9.95, pbk £4.95)

Social security

Directory for the Disabled Ann Darnbrough, Derek Kinrade (Woodhead-Faulkner, 3rd edn, 1981, hbk £9.25, pbk £5.50)

Disability Rights Handbook (Disability Alliance,* 1984, £2.00)

Guide to Housing Benefits Nick Raynsford, Peter McGurk (SHAC, London Housing Aid Centre,* 1983, £4.00)

National Welfare Benefits Handbook Janet Albeson, John Douglas (Child Poverty Action Group,* 13th edn, 1984, £3.00)

Rights Guide to Non-means-tested Social Security Benefits Mark Rowland, Roger Smith (Child Poverty Action Group,* 6th edn, 1984, £3.00)

Tolley's Social Security and State Benefits Jim Matthewman, Nigel Lambert (Tolley, 1984, £10.95)

Taxation

'Daily Mail' Income Tax Guide 1983–4 Ed. Kenneth Tingley (Harmsworth Publications, £1.00)

Hambro Capital Taxes and Estate Planning Guide W.I. Sinclair, P.D. Silke (Oyez Longman, 1982, £9.95)

Hambro Tax Guide 1983–4 Ed. Walter Sinclair (Oyez Longman, 1983, £9.95)

101 Ways of Saving Tax Elaine Baker, Bill Packer (*Sunday Telegraph*, 1984, £1.95)

Tolley's Capital Gains Tax Robert Wareham, Patrick Noakes (Tolley, 1983, £9.75)

Tolley's Capital Transfer Tax Robert Wareham, Jane Scollen (Tolley, 1983, £8.75)

Tolley's Practical Tax Guide Arnold Homer, Rita Burrows (Tolley, 1983, £10.95)

Wills

Right Way to Prove a Will Keith Best (Elliot Right Way Books, 1981, £0.85)

What to Do When Someone Dies (Consumers' Association,* 1984, £4.95)

Wills and Probate (Consumers' Association,* 1984, £4.95)

Write Your Own Will Keith Best (Elliot Right Way Books, 1978, £0.85)

Periodicals

Money Magazine (monthly) Subscription Office, Sweeny Bourke McAllister Ltd, 8a West Smithfield, London EC1A 9JR (£12.00 p.a., post free; back copies £0.95)

Money Management (monthly) Subscription Office, Minster House, Arthur Street, London EC4R 9AX (£38.50 p.a. 1st class post; £33.00 p.a. 2nd class post; back copies £2.75 inc. p. and p.)

Money Observer (monthly) Subscription Dept., 374 Wandsworth Road, London SW8 4TE (£14.50 p.a.; back copies £1.50)

Planned Savings (monthly) Subscription Office, Wootten Publications, 150–52 Caledonian Road, London N1 9RD (£32.00 p.a. 1st class post; £27.50 p.a. 2nd class post)

What Investment? (£18.60 p.a.), What Mortgage? (£16.20 p.a.), What Finance? (£25.20 p.a.), What Insurance? (£18.60 p.a.); all monthly and inc. p. and p.: Subscription Office, Financial Magazines Ltd, Consort House, 26–28 Queensway, London W2 3RX

Index